Not to the Manner Born

MEMOIRS AND OCCASIONAL PAPERS
Association for Diplomatic Studies and Training

In 2003, the Association for Diplomatic Studies and Training (ADST) created the Memoirs and Occasional Papers Series to preserve firsthand accounts and other informed observations on foreign affairs for scholars, journalists, and the general public. Sponsoring series publication is one of numerous ways in which ADST, a nonprofit organization founded in 1986, seeks to promote understanding of American diplomacy and those who conduct it. Others include the Foreign Affairs Oral History program and ADST's support for the training of foreign affairs personnel at the State Department's Foreign Service Institute.

Not to the Manner Born

Reflections of a Wife and Partner in the Foreign Service

Helen Lyman

Association for Diplomatic Studies and Training
Memoirs and Occasional Papers Series

NEW ACADEMIA PUBLISHING SCARITH

Washington, DC

New Academia Publishing/SCARITH Books, 2011

Printed in the United States of America

Library of Congress Control Number: 2010941047
ISBN 978-0-9828061-7-3 paperback (alk. paper)
ISBN 978-0-9828061-9-7 hardcover (alk. paper)

SCARITH   An imprint of New Academia Publishing
P.O. Box 27420, Washington, DC 20038-7420

NEW ACADEMIA PUBLISHING   www.newacademia.com
info@newacademia.com

Contents

Foreword

Helen Lyman came reluctantly to the world of diplomacy. She grew up with the image of making her adult home near her parents in San Francisco, and like her older brother and his family, coming each Friday night to her parents' home for dinner. When we became serious in high school, and I told her of my ambitions for a life in the Foreign Service, it almost ended our early romance. When I promised her not to spend all our lifetimes in faraway places, she relented.

In time she became almost more of a world traveler than I. But as she sets out in this memoir, she was not "to the manner born." And she meant that spelling of manner! Formality and ceremony did not impress her. Pretense, even in the service of better ends, was not her thing. Yet she wrote as she prepared the essays in this book, "Mostly it has been an exhausting but exhilarating ride that, had I to choose again (with the benefit of hindsight), I would choose again in a heartbeat." Her sense of humor made her able to step back and see the funnier side of even the most serious moments. Her purpose in writing this book was thus, originally, to "give the reader something to smile about. No one can have too many smiles in their life."

But the book morphed into something more. Increasingly, she examined not only the moments of her life abroad, but her whole life, and the meaning of all that around her. She explored it in both essay and poetry. It became a much more nuanced account, seasoned by the sadness of the illness that would not let her go. At the time of Helen's death, the book was still very much a work in progress, so it is presented as a collection of essays rather than a fully realized memoir.

I have been struck in the messages I have received since her death of her impact on the people in her life. In almost every message, people spoke to me of her warmth, her ready smile, her positive outlook on life, and her encouragement to others. She never engaged in bureaucratic rivalries, never got caught up in fights among friends or family. Instead she was always the one to keep people together and to foster cooperation. I cannot think of a single person in her lifetime who disliked her or ever feuded with her.

She made long, close friendships that extended over time and place. One special friend, Helen Seitz, we met when our children were small. The two of them stayed close even when we moved away. Later Helen Seitz would go with Helen to volunteer work, come to family events, and later, when my Helen could no longer drive, would on a moment's notice drive her to wherever – doctor and dentist appointments, shopping – and make an outing of it, going for lunch or some other fun place. They talked often on the phone, laughed and cried together. They were the "Two Helens."

Of course while she was indeed very positive on life, especially with those with whom she came into contact, I knew that there were times when the violence in the world, the unfairness, the inequities, depressed her. She threw herself into voluntary work whenever she could, whether for better government, for peace, or for causes of political progressiveness. I always remember our standing with our three small children in a long silent demonstration against the war in Vietnam, and when, heavy with carrying our second child, she insisted on standing for hours to view John Kennedy's casket in the U.S. Capitol rotunda. As she recounts in one of her essays, the violence in Israel had a deeply personal meaning for her. She could never understand the proclivity of men and nations for war.

Helen and I were married in 1957. We both graduated from the University of California, Berkeley, that year and headed to Cambridge, Massachusetts, where I was to pursue my studies for a Ph.D. (Helen had wanted me to accept an offer instead from Princeton University. She liked the idea of an address that read Mr. and Mrs. Princeton Lyman, Princeton University, Princeton, New Jersey). Helen soon discovered that her B.A. in Social Work did not qualify her for anything like the work she had anticipated. Her only offer was to check on the households of female welfare recipients to see if they were hiding a man somewhere, an act that would have made them ineligible for benefits. So instead she accepted a job as a bank teller, beginning a career in that field that would come back several times in the future. We had in so many ways a very good life. We were not without our troubles, and our periods of difficulty. But Helen was the solid rock in the marriage and in the family. She made it work. Forever, my children and I will love her for it.

Like many spouses of Foreign Service officers, Helen found her career interrupted time and again. It was frustrating for her. Her first priority was nevertheless our family. When, as she recounts in one of her essays, she embarked on a program and later career of family counseling, she made our home a far happier and less contentious one than would otherwise have been the case. Helen also insisted that we always have breakfast and dinner together, no matter what. When, at one period of my career, I was coming home as late as 9 or 10 o'clock each night, Helen would have the children wait for dinner (with snacks before to be sure, but still unhappy to be made to wait) so that we would always eat together.

Our overseas posts were not so many in terms of typical Foreign Service careers, but they were each in their way momentous. In South Korea, 1964–1967, we witnessed the beginning of that country's dramatic transformation from a desperately poor country to, over time, one of the strongest economies in the world. In Ethiopia, 1976–1978, we lived through one of the worst and bloodiest periods of the Marxist-military revolution that had overtaken that country. In Nigeria, 1986–1989 (Helen coming in the second year), we came to know the vibrancy and the woes of one of Africa's most important and dynamic countries. And in South Africa, 1992–1995, we became part of one of the outstanding stories of encouragement and progress in the 20th century, the ending of apartheid not through bloody civil war as many had predicted but through statesmanlike negotiation. There is no question that the South Africa experience was for Helen the crown jewel of her overseas experience, in a way making it all worthwhile.

Helen was determined in our overseas life to be her own person, the subject of her entertaining (but probably too self-deprecating) essay in this book on speaking to a diplomatic wives' seminar at the State Department. She was not content to be "wife of the

AID director," or later "the ambassador's wife." Thus in Ethiopia she began what became one of her lifetime joys—teaching, first kindergarten and later first grade. She would ever after describe herself as a first grade teacher, even when she was teaching State Department officers the ways and whims of computers. But uprooted time and again, she had to fall back on banking (to help us put our girls through college), being a teacher's aide, a temp in Montgomery County, Maryland, and finally an instructor in the State Department's computer training program.

As she recounted it, wondering why she had been asked to apply for that last job, she told the State Department recruiter that she knew nothing of computers, and was only a first grade teacher. "Wonderful," said the interviewer, "we have plenty of people who are experts in computers, but few who can relate to Foreign Service officers resistant to this stuff. First grade sounds just right." She was a terrific success, traveling to China, Israel, El Salvador, Botswana, Swaziland, Turkey, Switzerland, Ethiopia, and South Korea. I hear often from officers who say that she unlocked the mysteries of that technology and made them almost literate in it against their most basic instincts!

Helen never wavered from her hope that the time would come when I would stop being so busy and we would enjoy the fruits of a more settled life. It was not to happen. Shortly after retiring from the State Department in 1999, I began a nearly full-time career with various think tanks, teaching, and the like. It is not that we did not do some of the travel we had long talked about—a cruise to Alaska, another in the Mediterranean, trips to China, Japan, New Mexico, and Colorado, and of course every year to Israel to visit our daughter and her family there. But I was basically preoccupied with my work, and Helen soon realized that she would have to chart her own post-Department life. If there is a silver lining in my disappointing her hopes, it was that Helen turned to writing. And she found her voice.

She began with a writing course at the Writer's Center in Bethesda in 2003. In her first class, the students melded so well that they decided to continue meeting on their own. They rented a room at the Writer's Center and began meeting each Thursday. The remaining members do so to this day. The first half of the meeting they would write, then the second half read their work and have it critiqued. Soon they began following the meeting with lunch. The women in this group became one of the most important and supportive groups of friends in Helen's life. They encouraged her, sustained her in times of illness, gave her warmth and the generosity of their professionalism and their personalities. They were angels in Helen's life. She cherished that group as nothing else. She would take other courses, in writing autobiography, in poetry, in children's books. But nothing sustained her work as much as this group of friends and colleagues in the love of writing. Laura Golberg, a member of this group and one of Helen's closest friends, wrote the poem that closes this book.

It was a terrible act of fate that when we returned from our last overseas post in 1995 and had our final departmental check-ups, I was assigned to Helen's favorite doctor there and she to another. My doctor recommended a colonoscopy; hers did not. Two years later, Helen was diagnosed with colorectal cancer, and when surgery was performed, it was found to have metastasized to her liver. That began the long siege with cancer. Helen was determined to beat it. After surgery, she took six months of chemotherapy and against the odds (she was told that only 20 percent of patients responded to it), it seemed to work. We enjoyed a seven-year period of remission thereafter, thinking by the fifth year that she had passed the danger mark. During that time, Helen counseled colorectal cancer victims around the country, urging them not to despair from dire diagnoses, and to seek the best, and even the most aggressive treatments. She wrote a similar article in a cancer magazine.

But it was not to last. In 2005, the cancer returned, this time spreading through her chest. She underwent more surgery, then six months of terrible chemo treatment, devastating to her well-being. She enjoyed a short respite, of just feeling well and being grateful (see her essay "Thoughts"), only to be told later that the treatment had not worked. Her doctor gave her up, telling us she would die by the end of the year. We changed doctors.

At Georgetown University Hospital, we found John Marshall, a doctor who cared as much about quality of life as the medicine for treating it. Through him, we gained two more years. They were not easy ones. More chemo drained away her strength; radiation and an endless series of medications were almost bewildering. But it enabled us to enjoy an absolutely fantastic 50th wedding anniversary celebration which our daughters and grandchildren arranged. In November 2007, we took one more trip to South Africa, a country Helen absolutely loved. We had one more safari there (see her poem on the veldt), the best we had ever experienced. And Helen was able to realize one of her last goals, to see our oldest granddaughter graduate from college in May 2008.

Helen cursed the cancer. She hated that it was taking over her life. She fought it. Even when she was so weak that she needed a wheelchair and was weary most of the time, she signed up for not one but two more courses at the Writer's Center. I would come home and find her struggling to do the homework, fighting against fatigue. Nevertheless, she insisted that I drive her to the courses each week. After she passed away, I sent a note to one of her instructors telling her of Helen's death and how badly Helen had felt that she was often late and usually not fully prepared, but really had enjoyed the course. The instructor wrote me back that Helen had told her that, and had explained her condition but said that she wanted to go each week because she was determined that cancer would not rule her life.

On the night of July 5, 2008, Helen had a particularly bad night. By then she was in Home Hospice Care. I spent the night on the phone with the nurse trying to see what could be done. The next morning the nurse came and was able to make Helen comfortable. But she told me that the end was near.

Helen and I were both tennis players. Helen was not flashy but steady in defense and often fooled the opponents who underestimated her. We had a long tradition of each year sitting up in bed and watching the Wimbledon finals. In England the tradition is to serve strawberries during the finals. So we, as the broadcaster suggested, would have strawberries and enjoy "breakfast at Wimbledon."

Despite what the nurse had said, I turned on the finals scheduled for that morning. I so wanted Helen to wake up and have one more time watching them with me. But it was not to be. Early that afternoon, surrounded by two of our daughters and me, Helen slipped quietly away.

She died one day shy of our 51ˢᵗ wedding anniversary. This book was something she very much wanted to see to fruition. I hope each of you find in it both pleasure and inspiration.

Princeton N. Lyman

Helen and Princeton in Maryland, 2007, our Golden Anniversary year.

Preface

Perhaps, finding the humor in the experiences I had as the wife of a diplomat was my way of maintaining (or giving the appearance of maintaining) some semblance of sanity in a world I was definitely not born to participate in.

Getting ready for some formal event where my husband is going to host high-level officials, I am still amazed at how calmly and quickly he dons his tux and looks great, doesn't worry about the speech he will give (usually not even bothering to write it out), checks over the seating arrangements, gives instructions to the embassy staff who are required to arrive early, and is standing at his spot in the reception line ahead of schedule. There is no doubt in my mind that he was born to be an ambassador. Even his name, Princeton, seems to imply comfortably mixing with world leaders.

Although I have learned to leave domestic duties that normally would be mine to the professional house staff, and although I will have nothing to do at that event but smile and eat, I am a nervous wreck. I have never gotten over being shy, learned to make conversation with people I don't know (this is even harder for me if they are famous), or to remember names. At a reception, I cannot walk up to a group of people and somehow join the group. I often feel that I missed the boat with how I dressed for the event. I was not born to be an ambassador's wife. As I said: his name is Princeton; my name is Helen.

Family

Born in America

I was born in San Francisco in 1935 during my parents' first year in the United States. They had escaped from Nazi Germany along with my two brothers, six-year-old Don, and two-year-old Egan, and a teenage cousin. My brother Egan died during the voyage and was buried at sea.

My mother always described her childhood in Germany as idyllic. She said she led a charmed life as the adored, spoiled, and protected youngest child in a large, loving well-to-do family. With her tiny bone structure and deep blue eyes too large for her small face, she merely had to smile to always get her way at home, at school, and even with her friends. She knew, instinctively, when and how far to push, and so life as she was growing up could not have been better. She had always been a "teacher's pet" and enjoyed being held up as an example to the other children. With a beautiful singing voice, she was even picked to lead the singing of the Christmas carols, with no thought of her being Jewish. On the Jewish holiday of Purim, the Jewish children dressed up in costumes and showed them off to their neighbors and received admiration and sweets.

She lived near the French border in a town that was too small to make it onto the maps of Germany. World War I began when she was a young teenager, and she was incredibly proud of her handsome oldest brother as he marched off to war in his uniform. He came home on furlough with gifts and stories of teaching German songs to the enemy French soldiers doing guard duty on the other side of the fence he was guarding, while they taught him French songs. The war did not sound so bad in his telling, and so his death at the hands of a French soldier who had not heard the news that the war was over was devastating.

One story she told of her early married life showed how close the family circle was. A month before her second son's birth she had her hair cut. It was a family decision, involving parents and in-laws, finally made because all reluctantly agreed that, with two children, she would not have time to care for the soft golden brown hair that cascaded to her waist. On the day it was scheduled for cutting, my father went to work as usual but then came running into the beauty parlor to say he had changed his mind. But he arrived too late — the hair had been braided to make the cutting easier and one braid already lay on the black-and-white checkered floor.

While my mother recovered from her second son's birth, the nuns at the hospital treated her kindly, even more kindly than their Catholic patients. For they knew, what she did not yet realize, that the infant sleeping so peacefully in her arms could not survive. He was born with intestinal problems that inhibited his absorption of nutrients.

When she left the hospital with her baby and all the complicated instructions of the extra care he would need, she was determined to keep him alive. And for two years, in spite of the fourteen doctors she and her husband visited hoping for a better prognosis, she did just that. This child now took all her time and attention but grew and smiled and talked and walked and had a sunny disposition.

The strength and determination she mustered to keep her son alive and happy imprisoned them both in a fantasy world where life revolved around his care and trips to hospitals and those foods and activities that gave him pleasure.

One fall day, the Nazis hammered a large wooden sign on the door of the family store. In their small town, the sign was ignored and life went on as before. When, months later, the Nazis returned with a larger sign and hammered closed the front door, life still didn't change except that customers had to use the back door. By the time the store finally was shut down, however, my mom was becoming a bit concerned. But, she willed herself to ignore the new dangers that faced her family. When her six-year-old son was teased or hit at school because he was Jewish, she comforted him but could not face the seriousness of the threats.

But then came the day my father went to the barbershop for a shave and saw a swastika under his barber's white smock. He walked out of the shop and onto the front page of the local newspaper where he was described as "the Jew Ermann." He decided then that they would have to leave and started working on getting out.

My mother refused to leave. When her uncle in America, seeing the problems in Germany more clearly from a distance than German Jews saw it from within, implored her to come to America, she still refused. Her father was ill and her mother would not leave him so she dismissed all suggestions of flight as impossible. When my father's American uncle came to Germany to plead his case and offered a job and a home in America, it made no difference. She would stay put and nurse her child and comfort her parents.

So, her desperate husband came up with a plan that he felt necessary to save his family. He persuaded the uncle to tell my mother that he believed the doctors in America might save her son. This was a lie, but the uncle went along with the plan. My mother, in her constant quest to find a cure for her child, grabbed this new slim hope for a miracle in a new land.

The uncle had no trouble securing the necessary paperwork needed to arrive in America, but the German government was reluctant to grant permission for the family to leave the country. When my father had tickets for a ship leaving in a week, he still couldn't get the exit papers he needed. He finally resorted to calling a high-level German government official—a longtime friend. Upon hearing Dad's story, this friend promised to have the necessary paperwork ready the next day. But my dad had to promise to board the ship that same day, even though it was not yet ready to sail. The friend also told my father not to call him if anything went wrong. If another call came, he would deny even knowing Dad. The following day Mom, Dad, my two brothers, and a cousin boarded the ship.

They sailed on the MS *Takoma* from Hamburg on New Year's Eve 1934 for the 35-day trip. It had seemed an appropriate start to a new year and a new life. The ship, although a freighter, was adequate for the journey. It was part of a fleet of freighters on the Hamburg-America Line—all named after northwest American cities. These ships were designed to carry a small number—less than 200 passengers—and provided comfortable accommodation, good meals, pleasant staff, and a doctor. It was not the *Queen Mary* but it did provide an inflatable swimming pool. My brother Don was the only one who didn't get seasick.

The ship's first stop was at the Panama Canal and they disembarked and took a walk. They had to laugh in spite of themselves as a man they could not understand tried to get my dad to buy a shirt. The man, in his great effort to make himself understood, pulled at the shirt, supposedly to show its great endurance, but the shirt ripped in two. They could not in any case afford any purchases. Hitler, at that point was allowing Jews to leave and take their possessions but only $100 of their money.

My brother Don still remembers the night our brother Egan died. He said that, over seventy years later, he could still hear our mother's scream. He was awakened from a deep sleep by the sound coming through the door of their adjoining cabins. Egan's death was especially tragic since our mother had only agreed to go to America for his benefit. In later years the whole family would have to reflect that this child's illness saved not only her life and the life of his father and brother and cousin. The children, grandchildren, and great-great grandchildren who would never have been born must now number in the hundreds.

My mother's first year in America was hard and lonely. She couldn't speak English. She spent much of her time crying—so much so that when Don came home from school one day and saw her weeping in front of a picture of the baby, he turned the picture to face the wall. He couldn't know how that would affect his mother, but she realized what she was doing to her family and did not turn the picture around.

Accustomed to living in comfortable homes with servants, my mother had to learn to clean and cook in a small bungalow. But she knew she was fortunate that her American aunt came over daily to teach her to shop and cook and make her way in the new foreign land. At first, my mother was appalled when she saw people buying corn in the grocery store—in Germany only pigs ate corn. She felt repulsed watching a woman in a restaurant eat an artichoke and thought Americans must be barbarians. She reluctantly put away her son's hand-knitted wardrobe when he complained about being teased at school. Fortunately the aunt immediately bought him an

American wardrobe. Eventually, the times she longed to be back in Germany became fewer.

She and my father had arrived with very little money, so she watched every penny to help her husband save enough to start a business. In order to save bus fare she walked to her doctor's appointments and even to the hospital to give birth to me.

I once asked my brother if our dad had gotten her pregnant in order to help her get over Egan's death.

"Yes," he said, "and you did the trick!

Branching Out

I suppose it isn't surprising that my mother was overprotective of me. When I was in the first grade, I remember her standing over me at breakfast and making sure I ate my cereal and drank the orange juice she had squeezed for me. Before school, she combed and braided my long hair and tied it with white ribbons. She showed her love by doing everything for me rather than teaching me to do anything for myself.

I met Princeton in high school, and he started taking care of me in much the same way my mother did. In college I moved right into a nice Jewish sorority where all the young women came from the same type of environment as I did. We never questioned having a housemother who lived with us and enforced the rules of study time, lockout at 10:00 P.M. on weekdays and 2:00 a.m. on weekends. As a pledge I was assigned a big sister.

After my marriage at 21, I became a traditional wife and mother, spending all my time making life as easy as I could for my husband and our three daughters. It simply never occurred to me that I could or should have any kind of a life of my own. I actually asked my husband's permission for any small purchase I wanted to make or activity I wanted to enjoy.

Then, when my husband was away on one of his many foreign trips, at a friend's suggestion I joined a child-raising study group. It was my first ever act of independence. I didn't discuss it with him, didn't question my right to spend the money, and didn't have him there to give me directions to the location of the group meetings.

What a wondrous change this study group made in my life—the final result of which sent me back to school for a master's degree in education and counseling.

The first study group, based on the Rudolf Dreikurs book *Children, the Challenge*, changed my relationship with my daughters in all sorts of ways. Just twice pulling the car over and waiting for them to stop fighting ended car fighting forever. When Princeton and I took our dinner plates to the living room instead of giving a child attention for misbehaving at the table, it turned dinnertime into a pleasant experience—at least until they were teenagers. Bedtime also changed completely when we stopped insisting the girls be in bed at a certain time. We had the usual playtime, bath time, and story time routine. and then we kissed them goodnight and left it to them to decide when to sleep. When no one came into their room in response to noise and radios and lights, those things seemed to lose their appeal and the girls went to sleep when they were tired.

My second study group was based on Dreikurs's *The Challenge of Marriage*—a real eye-opener. Soon, I was leading groups, counseling using the Dreikurs theories, and then I moved on to get my master's degree.

After the training I had received to become a counselor for the Dreikurs group, I felt guilty about leaving to go back to school. The psychiatrist who ran the center smiled at my apology and said that that was, actually, the purpose of the training. It wasn't until years later that I understood his meaning. All the training in childcare, marriage relations, and counseling techniques was not only for the families we counselors could help—but for the study group leaders and counselors themselves.

My Father

I had the best dad, although I know if I start to write about him it won't sound that way. I can't say I really knew him—he, and therefore I, grew up in homes where, by tradition, the father earned the money and the mother took care of the house and raised the kids. Having arrived from Germany just about penniless, bringing home the kosher bacon meant Dad left the apartment before I woke up and arrived home after I was asleep. In those days in any case, men didn't even hold babies—much less feed them, give them a bath, or, heaven forbid, change a diaper.

As I grew up, Dad worked six days a week, and Sundays were scheduled for him to visit customers in their homes. After we acquired a car, the family sometimes got an outing out of his Sunday appointments; he would drop us off to enjoy a park while he worked. Some Sundays there were no appointments and we actually had family picnics and drives to the countryside. Family vacations were planned with other families who had kids, so even then I never really talked to my dad.

I seem to remember only these bad times—a spanking or being taken in the ocean when I was little and scared to death. My feelings were hurt when I was a young wife and he refused my dessert because he was on a diet but then ate some store-bought dessert. When he visited me, he called my brother every day, but when he was back home in San Francisco, he only called me once a week.

I do remember some arguments about prejudice and have only lately come to realize that, though by my standards he didn't measure up well, he really was quite liberal for his time.

So what made him so great? One thing was his courage and honesty. When my father was fourteen years old, his father was wounded in World War I. As the eldest of four children, he had to quit school and run the family business. There went his dream of becoming a doctor. Then there was the time, which I've already mentioned, when he was getting a shave, saw a swastika under the barber's smock, and walked out of the shop. This was reported in the local newspaper, and he had to hide and get out of Germany quickly. After arriving in the United States, he worked night and day to support his family. Through all this, Dad was the eternal optimist, who tried to keep us all positive about the future.

Though we so seldom spoke—and when we did it was often an argument—he said two of the most helpful things anyone ever said to me. The first was on the day I was married when he said: "This will always be a home for you." The second was when he thought he might die, and he told me not to grieve because he had had such a wonderful life.

My Stepmother-in-law

My first conversation with my stepmother-in-law was rather bizarre. It seemed she didn't want to participate in my wedding or stand in the reception line in case someone thought she was actually old enough to be my husband's real mother. She did finally consent, having been convinced by a clever uncle that she looked so young that no one could possibly think that, and it would be a shame if people didn't get to go through the reception line and see how pretty she was. All the family agreed that no one would introduce her as Princeton's mother.

Princeton was twelve when his mother died. About two years after her death, his father, Arthur, took a trip around the world. While he was in Israel, he became friends with and then married the young woman who cleaned his hotel room. Her name was Shoshana. These two people could not have had more different agendas for their married life.

Arthur was truthful when he told Shoshana that he had a large home in San Francisco, but less so about the fact that two of his children were still teenagers and living at home, with a strong-willed live-in housekeeper, and that, instead of being in the wholesale grocery business as he had told her, he in fact had a small grocery store. Shoshana was rather astonished to see all six children on hand to meet her when she disembarked in San Francisco.

Arthur had been looking for someone to run his household and help in the store. Shoshana had been looking for someone to get her to America and then bring all her relatives over as well. She soon discovered that the funds for this would not be provided willingly. She found working in the store perfectly distasteful. She stayed for a few years, managed to spend most of her husband's money on travel and clothing, and when it was all gone, she disappeared without a trace. Rumor had it that she was in Los Angeles.

Cindy's Wedding

There are unexpected phone calls, and then there are really unexpected phone calls that knock your socks off and leave you speechless.

That's the kind I got one very ordinary Sunday morning while my youngest daughter, Lori, then 17, and I were munching our breakfast bagels and enjoying the fact that we could stay indoors, cozy and warm, and enjoy the snow through the picture windows of our family room. I was in the United States, so that Lori could spend her senior year with her friends, and not in Nigeria where Princeton was living and serving as the American ambassador. Our middle daughter, Sheri, was married and lived near us. Our oldest daughter, Cindy, was spending the year in Israel, working as a nurse and learning the culture and language.

I was enjoying my job, my time with family and friends, and, while a bit lonely, was not unhappy. I had, in fact, recently returned from a whirlwind three-week trip to Nigeria where I had spent my time being introduced to at least a million people. I had also barely survived the strain of hosting Mrs. George Shultz, wife of the U.S. secretary of state, for an entire day. She was delightful, but I was still a wreck.

While I was in Nigeria, I had had a job interview and was delighted that I would be teaching first grade in the American school when I eventually joined my husband. I love teaching six-year-olds, and I was glad to have an excuse not to spend my days at meetings, luncheons, and bridge parties.

When the phone rang, I had no premonition that this would be other than a routine call. Even when I heard Cindy's voice from

Israel, I thought it would just be a call to say, "Hi." She did say "Hi," but she also said, "I'm getting married in May. Can you and Dad and everyone come?"

"You're getting married? In four months? But whom are you marrying? Is he an Israeli? Where will you live? Where did you meet him? What does he do?" etc. etc. etc.

She seemed quite surprised by my surprise. "Didn't you get my letter? I wrote that I had gone out with Chanina, enjoyed his company, and was planning to see him again."

"Yes, I got the letter, but seeing someone once and saying you will see him again doesn't usually count as an engagement announcement."

"Well, you know, in the religious community you don't date— you just meet someone a friend thinks is right for you, go to a public place, talk, and you don't see each other again unless you think it could work out into a marriage. So, when I said that I would see him again, that was a hint we might marry."

"Oh, O.K., well it's nice to hear you sound so happy. I'll call Dad and I'm sure we'll figure a way to get there for the wedding."

When I got off the phone, I couldn't help wondering how they could decide after seeing each other twice that this would work out.

They followed their tradition, were never alone together and never touched each other for the four months between meeting and marriage. Twenty years and eight children later, I can't find any flaws in their approach to selecting a lifelong partner!

Will It Ever End?

We looked back at our two-year-old granddaughter, holding her mommy's hand, her smiling dimpled face framed by the rifles of the two Israeli soldiers walking in front of her. Princeton and I both noticed that moment and wondered if it was a sign of what her future would be like. It was 1989.

Two years later, it seems to have been an indicator. When the first Iraq war broke out and missiles were landing in Israel, we telephoned our daughter Cindy—who now used her Hebrew name Tova—then living in Jerusalem, and suggested she bring her family home during the fighting.

"We are home," she informed me indignantly.

During the war between Israel and Hezbollah in Lebanon in 2006, when we heard on CNN that Safed, where she is now living, was the target of the first rocket attacks, we called again. Cindy and her family did not know anything about the missiles. While we were on the phone, the Israeli sirens went off and my daughter said that she and her family would go to the shelter near their home. Later, for a short time, Cindy and her children left the city for a safer one, but returned even while the fighting continued.

This morning, CNN reported an outbreak of Arab-on-Arab violence in the Gaza Strip and some exchange of rockets with Israel. I have not heard of the city they mentioned, but it wasn't Safed; so I took my shower and went to my writing group. I tried to ignore the additional information that Hamas was threatening to resume suicide bombings on the streets and buses and in the cafes of Israel.

What can a mother and grandmother do from this distance? Are we supposed to butt out even when it is a matter of life and death?

On the other hand, I must admit I am not the least bit afraid when visiting Israel. Life in Safed goes on as usual. Kids run to catch the school bus, squabble a bit, snack, play with friends, put off doing their homework, try not to get noticed if they aren't eating the "healthy" food, hope no one notices the chore they "forgot" to do, sneak in a little extra time before sleeping, and all the other things kids do.

Moms go shopping, do the laundry, change the diapers, referee the arguments, make sure homework is done and put in the backpack, and cook, cook, cook. Dads help moms and do all the stuff that needs doing outside of the house.

When Princeton and I are in Israel we fit right in with the other tourists visiting their children, filling up the restaurants, buying Israeli gifts to bring back to the United States, and sightseeing in that beautiful and historic country. We hardly notice that there are soldiers with rifles carelessly thrown over their shoulders on the streets, on the buses, and in front of stores and restaurants.

But when we come back to the United States and watch CNN, we worry.

Apology

How do you apologize to someone who is not here? Even when he *was* here, he didn't get to live long enough to learn to understand, or even to talk. Eight months is not long to be around, but even had he lived he would not have understood my apology.

His name was Kevin and he was my son. He had Down syndrome in the days when "those children" were rarely given a chance to live and love and grow in their own homes. In those days, there were no miracle drugs to cure so many childhood infections. Children with Down syndrome usually did not survive childhood because of their inability to fight off such infections.

So, Kevin was placed with a nice lady who took care of "children like him." She, not his mother, picked him up when he was ready to leave the hospital; and she, not his mother, put him in a cradle next to her bed so she would hear if his breathing changed during the night. She would have known what to do; I would have panicked.

My husband and I made the three-hour drive to see and hold Kevin every other Sunday. He would be dressed in clothes we had purchased for him and he always looked clean and cute and content. He seemed to enjoy having us hold him and feed him. It was easy to make him smile and laugh.

Then, we would give him back to the nice lady to change his diaper and give him his bath. Afterwards, we would drive home guiltily, stopping for dinner on the way and trying to feel glad that he at least seemed alert and happy.

We asked if we might take Kevin home for a weekend, but then we agreed to wait until the weather turned warmer and he would be less likely to get ill. How strange to be asking permission to spend time with your own child; to actually be grateful when allowed simply to hold and feed him.

And then came that Sunday morning—a Sunday we were planning to visit Kevin. The phone rang while we were still asleep. This time, our visit would be to the hospital instead of the home where he lived. Kevin put up a brave struggle, living in his oxygen tent longer than the doctors expected, but he never really had a chance.

So, this is a 44-year-late apology to my son. I am sorry I didn't have the self-confidence and courage to take you home from the hospital. Your dad and I love you and I still think of you almost every day.

Foreign Service

South Korea

First Diplomatic Assignment 1964–1967

She just kept talking and talking and telling me things I knew I had to know, but I didn't hear a word. All my fears were coming true as the car inched its way through the crowded streets of Seoul, South Korea. This was the first time I had accompanied my husband Princeton to an overseas posting. My two babies and I had been whisked out of the airport and into Peggy's car. Her husband was a coworker and friend of my husband but we had never met. There was a driver in the front seat and the four of us sat in the back. And where was Princeton? Oh yes, he was in a car with that good friend who had suggested him for this new job. That friend, as I found out later, was serving him martinis while his driver proceeded in the same direction as our car.

I had never been in a third world country, which is what South Korea was in 1964, before it started its successful transformation, after a devastating war that left it divided from the north and struggling. Peggy cheerfully talked on and on, oblivious to my unsuccessful efforts to comfort my hungry, tired babies, both in need of a diaper change. I was trying to make a good impression at this first encounter with diplomatic niceties; but, not only did my children distract me, but so did the amazing sounds and smells and scenes moving slowly past the car windows.

The traffic was not crawling along because of other cars, but because of people and animals and bicycles. I felt sad for an ox being pulled along by a ring through its nose. I felt even sadder for a fragile-looking Korean man carrying a huge load on his back on what I later learned was called an A-frame. It was a wood and bamboo contraption strapped to his back and so loaded he was bent double with the weight of it—or maybe he was bent double to keep things from falling off.

At least we had made it to Seoul: a feat that at times had seemed beyond me.

The first hurdle was back home in Virginia trying to find babysitters so I could attend a compulsory two-week course on how to be a good Foreign Service wife. Much of the course was devoted to such important matters as how to make "calls" on wives of my husband's bosses and on other foreign wives. I learned what my calling cards should say, and dutifully ordered them. I learned the length of time a visit should last and what to do if the person was not at home when I called. I learned, later, that this custom was not followed in Seoul and, in fact, not in any of the posts to which we were later assigned. I learned when to wear gloves, though I never needed them in all my diplomatic experience.

I also learned that, before the packers came, I was to sort our family possessions into various piles destined for airfreight or sea freight or storage or to be left for us to pack and take along. I wasn't sufficiently warned that several teams of packers would arrive at the same time so that it would be impossible to keep an eye on what was being packed. Predictably, our garbage can, complete with thrown-out food, went by airfreight, and the stroller we needed for the trip went by sea.

Then, there was the shopping for three years' worth of clothing and shoes. What fun it was to estimate who would need what and in what sizes in which seasons! And our meager bank account had to cover china and glasses for entertaining. Fortunately, we had gotten enough flatware as wedding gifts.

Then came the delight of flying from Washington, D.C., to Seoul with two small children. (Those were the days before jet travel.) The first leg was to visit my parents in San Francisco. That turned out to be as joyful as one could hope for while trying to keep two small ones from messing up my parents' ultraclean home and having my mom let us know how sad we made her by traveling so far away.

An overnight in Hawaii was pleasant enough until we almost missed our plane to Japan. Rushing to catch the plane with our arms full of carry-on luggage and a nine-month-old infant, we encountered a huge puddle that stretched all across the path. Our two-year-old daughter Cindy refused to get her new shoes wet by stepping in the puddle. No coaxing, bribing, or threats could move her; but eventually Princeton and I each shifted our loads precariously to free one hand and we grabbed Cindy's hands and swung her over the puddle. The flight to Japan was not bad, as we were well equipped with diapers and bottles and toys and the girls slept for much of it.

Our overnight in Tokyo was pleasurable, and we decided a walk the next morning would do us all good. We were amazed to see long lines of Japanese waiting at many locations. We thought it was admirable that they got to work so long before businesses even opened. Later we learned that they were actually in line to purchase tickets for the Olympics, and we were relieved that they were not as terribly conscientious and uptight as we had thought.

Princeton decided that, since it was only a short flight to Seoul, we should abandon carrying all those diapers and bottles and toys so we would make a better impression on whomever would meet our plane. This might have been a great idea, but as soon as we got settled for the flight, with the baby sound asleep, all passengers were asked to leave the plane because of a mechanical problem that would take some time to fix.

Our happily napping little one was now screaming, so our family was put in a separate room to await departure from Japan. As time went on, Princeton, who spoke no Japanese, had to venture out into the airport and try to find diapers and a few of the other objects we had jettisoned in order to make a good and uncluttered first impression in Seoul. I managed to get the baby back to sleep and was reading to Cindy while she was drinking some juice and sitting comfortably with her shoes off. Then an excited Japanese airline worker barged into the room. Though I couldn't understand him, I did figure out that the plane was ready to take off without our family. While he was rushing around throwing things into the diaper bag, I could not make him understand that one of our group was at large in the airport and that I didn't want to leave. Fortunately, Princeton (without the diapers) arrived before the worker walked off with Cindy in one arm and her shoes in the other hand with me refusing to pick up the baby and follow him. Once my husband had arrived, we ran to the plane, whose propellers were already whirring.

So, that is how I now found myself crawling along in a hot car, wide-eyed at the sights and smells of a teeming city like nothing I had ever seen, trying to soothe my unhappy children and trying to be polite to a woman I would have dearly loved to ask to please shut up.

Because our flight had been so delayed, we now had only about two hours before a required appearance at a dinner party in our honor. This was the kind of situation I had dreaded about Foreign Service life. I must now leave my already traumatized children with a nanny I had known for only two hours. We did manage to take a quick shower and set up the cribs, and get the children fed and asleep. My mind never did attend the party; it stayed in my new home with my sleeping babies. As soon as dinner was over, the nanny called, seemed angry with us, and said we must come now as she had to leave in order to make curfew. There was a great flurry of activity as people called the nanny and asked her to stay overnight. When she refused, they tried to figure out other plans so we could "enjoy" the rest of the party. I did try to hide my glee at this excuse to escape.

The girls seemed to recover from this traumatic introduction to the life of children of diplomatic parents. I'm not sure I ever did.

First Cocktail Party

It was the first cocktail party I had to attend in my new role as the wife of an American diplomat, a moment I had been dreading. Immediately, I could tell that on an enjoyment scale of one to ten, this was going to be minus 1,000. I was in a room full of strangers chatting at a decibel level that gave me a headache, holding a drink so stiff that I couldn't swallow it, and breathing in enough second-hand smoke to barbeque a four-inch-thick steak.

I was dressed in the appropriate cocktail dress and had paid to have my ponytail put into a more suitable style. I tried, really tried, for the proper wife-of-a-diplomat behavior. I reminded myself that I must not be seen talking to another American—I was there to make the Koreans love Americans.

I dutifully avoided the four or five fellow wives I had met during the few days we had been in country, took a deep breath, and gathered up the courage to speak to a Korean-looking young lady who, like me, was standing alone and looking somewhat miserable.

This turned out to be quite pleasant—she was obviously happy to have someone to talk to. We exchanged names and talked about our children a bit. Then I realized that she was a Chinese-American spouse in the same predicament I was.

Seoul

I have known Seoul, the capital of South Korea, in three different ways. The most recent was in 1995, when I spent five weeks there teaching a new computer program to U.S. government employees. I enjoyed all the comforts and excitement of a thoroughly modern city complete with metal and glass skyscrapers, shopping malls, every variety of restaurant, well-dressed people rushing to work, traffic jams, and a clean, efficient subway system that offered a safe way to cross streets, and more shopping and restaurants, in addition to its transportation services. This modern Seoul retained only a few Korean structures with graceful slanted roofs and colorful walls. These seemed to have been kept mostly for tourists' photographs. While there were many nightclubs, to experience Korean music and dancing one had to go to "Korea House," which was just for tourists and had electronic devices to translate into English what was visible on stage.

The second Seoul I knew was the one with dirt roads and ramshackle shacks that once were the homes and shops of the South Koreans after the destruction of the Korean War. No trace of them is seen today among the gleaming buildings above the efficient subway.

A third Seoul was on the army complex where we lived when Princeton was stationed there from 1964 to 1967. This Seoul was almost an American suburb. Homes such as the one my family was assigned could be found in any town in the United States, with three bedrooms, two bathrooms, a kitchen, and a living room with a dining ell. The only difference might be the addition of a large laundry room, where a nanny would sleep if there were small children and parents who might have to stay out past the 10 o'clock curfew imposed on Koreans.

I could take my kids to a well-stocked commissary and buy, at very reasonable prices, everything we needed, though not quite everything we might like. One difference from a supermarket at home was that the ambassador's wife had issued a decree that American females could not wear pants in the commissary. The PX was not of much use to American wives. Things seemed to find their way to the Korean black market before we even knew the shipment had come in.

When we arrived in Seoul, we did not, like some people we knew, want to see only the American-style world of an army complex. So, shortly after our arrival, and before we had learned any Korean, we set out with two other newly arrived couples to have a meal in the downtown area. We were told of a Korean restaurant that served *bulgogi*—a beef dish that would be cooked at our table so we would know that it was safe to eat. We were also told that if we stuck to this and rice and drank hot tea or cold sodas, we should be OK.

So we set out, feeling a bit superior to those who didn't venture out. We found the restaurant with no trouble, gave some money to the beggars that surrounded our car, and caused a fair amount of commotion when we entered the restaurant. We had learned the Korean words for rice, tea, Fanta, *bulgogi*, and beer.

Since we were being treated as honored guests, we received some extra foods. We tried to be polite and yet only eat what seemed well cooked. We could also eat a cabbage-based salad called *kimchi*, because it was well fermented. It was so hot—as in spicy hot—that it would take us over a year of practice to actually enjoy it.

So, here sat six large Americans at a small restaurant, being served by smiling Koreans while the few other customers frankly stared at us. Our raw *bulgogi* was set out on a small stove at our table, and we watched it as our rice and drinks were served. Other customers then watched *us* while we watched the *bulgogi* turn crisp, and crisper, and crisper. We whispered to each other about what to do, when we noticed people at another table clap. The waitress then went to that table and turned the meat over. So, we clapped, and the waitress came and looked forlorn at the sight of our meat that had been burned to a crisp. Fortunately we got a second try.

Betty Kim

On Tuesdays, my friends and fellow Foreign Service spouses Françoise and Bettina and I devoted the day to helping Jane and her husband at the Holt orphanage, which was an hour and a half outside Seoul. A driver picked us up in his rickety pick-up truck and we bounced along on the unpaved dusty roads that took us there. Jane would meet the truck with great enthusiasm, which seemed way over what was warranted by the little work we did there. By the time we were served tea and lunch and made conversation, we were only with the children around two hours. But we knew that part of our contribution was to provide Jane with American company.

We greatly admired the work Jane was doing. Because the Koreans believed that babies who had white or black blood mixed with Korean blood must have had a prostitute for a mother, they were very happy to have Jane come through the Korean orphanage, pick out what looked like mixed-blood babies, and take them away. Jane took any baby who had a feature that might possibly not be Korean. In the Korean orphanage, 80 percent of the babies died. Those that went to the Holt orphanage had a chance of being selected to go to the United States for adoption.

One Tuesday, I was holding Betty Kim, a five-month-old. She had been selected for adoption by an African-American couple, but she was not thriving when offered food and care. She was scheduled to go the very next day to a Korean family who would be paid to fatten her up for the long flight to the United States. Jane was afraid that the baby would not live through the night, but assured us that if one of us would take her overnight and hold her she would recover.

I was wary of taking on this responsibility. First of all, I had two small children of my own and worried about bringing some sort of infection or disease home. Also, Betty Kim did look as if she could not live through the night; the thought of her dying in my home, with my children there, was especially frightening.

Jane had the type of strong personality that usually gets its way. She assured me the baby had been thoroughly checked for TB and other illnesses. She also was quite emphatic about the fact that if the baby were held, the diarrhea would stop and she would begin to eat. Jane gave me the address of where to take her the next morning.

So, I arrived home with a sick baby that I did not let my children see. My housekeeper let me know, in no uncertain terms, that she didn't approve and thought I was crazy. I didn't want to put the baby down, so Princeton was in for quite a shock when he came home for dinner.

For hours, Betty Kim continued to refuse the bottle, continued to have diarrhea, did not move in my arms, and made small weak moans every few minutes. I was sure she was dying.

Then, the diarrhea stopped and she took a small amount from the bottle. There was no miraculous cure, but she lived through the night and seemed a bit more alert. It was with great relief that I handed her over to the Korean family the next day.

It was years later, when speaking to the wife of an American businessman who lived in Korea and volunteered to take Korean orphans with her on her visits to the United States, that I put two and two together and realized that on one such trip this lady had taken a chubby and demanding Betty Kim to be adopted in America.

Rain

After four years of living in furnished (at least that's how they advertised themselves) apartments while Princeton went to graduate school, we had moved to Virginia, close to the State Department, where Princeton got a real job with a real paycheck. We rented a real one-bedroom apartment on the tenth floor of a new high-rise. It had a wonderful large window in the living room. Coming from San Francisco, Princeton and I had never experienced wild southern thunderstorms before. After the first such storm, we rushed out to buy a recording of Edgar Allen Poe stories and spent subsequent storms curled up on the sofa with the lights out, drinks in our hands, listening to the Poe stories. You can't beat that.

During the drought in South Africa, the afternoon sky would darken, the thunder would start, and then the sun would come out with not one precious raindrop to show for all that fierce-looking sky. After two years of drought, we had our first real rain, and everyone came out into it, laughed at getting all wet, and then went back to their offices still soaked.

While Princeton was in the USAID mission in South Korea, the country was experiencing a severe drought. In such a poor country, rain was literally a matter of life or death. So Princeton went through the long process of seeking drought relief aid to South Korea. Just when the aid was about to start, the rains finally came. And they came and they came and they came. After several days of this, a South Korean official phoned Princeton to ask about the status of the drought aid request.

"Well," said my husband, "given what has been coming down the past few days, I haven't been pressing Washington about it."

"Please," said the official, "just change the word 'drought' to 'flood,' because that is what we need the aid for now."

So Princeton sent a cable to Washington, changing his request for drought relief to flood relief. Washington actually was accommodating, and the aid came through without the AID office having to prepare a whole new set of papers.

Ethiopia 1976-1978

An Inauspicious Beginning

We arrived in Ethiopia in the early morning after an overnight flight from Rome. It was our first assignment in Africa, and our youngest daughter, who was seven years old, was relieved when we were driven up to a large house. She had in her mind that in Africa we would be sleeping in a tent in the wild (she only told us these fears years later). Princeton was taking over as USAID director, replacing our good friend John Withers.

It was pouring rain that morning. We were tired so, once settled in, we took a nap. We were wakened by the house staff a few hours later and urged to come outside. Next to the house, the pounding rains had turned a small spring into a raging river. The flood was carrying down pieces of roofing from nearby smaller houses, and an occasional animal floated by. It was an unsettling sight.

After a few minutes, one of the house staff turned to us, looking dour, and said, "This never happened when the Withers were here."

A One-of-a-Kind Bat Mitzvah

When our family learned that Princeton had been offered the job as AID director in Ethiopia, we were full of all the usual questions. When would we go? How long would we stay? What would we need to take with us? What could we buy there? What is the climate? What is there to do for fun? Will we be in danger? What kind of medical care is provided? How many Americans are there? Can we take the dog? The list of questions was endless. The most important questions, for our family, with children aged 6, 12, and 13, were about the school. It was not until we were able to verify the fact that there was an excellent American school that went from K through 12 that we agreed to consider the move.

Besides all the usual concerns, we had a unique one. Our 12-year-old daughter, Sheri, had started preparing for her bat mitzvah, which was scheduled for the coming December, when she would turn 13. So my husband sent a letter to the only Jewish temple in the capital, Addis Ababa, and asked if they could accommodate this important and special event. The answer was a not-very-enthusiastic yes. It seemed this temple was Orthodox and did not believe that girls should even be allowed inside the chapel, much less read from the Torah, as our daughter was planning to do. But, since this was the only temple available and Sheri was already studying the portion she would recite, they reluctantly agreed.

Sheri now had to prepare herself in only two months. So, between her usual activities, the extra shopping, the shots, and the farewells, she had to have a crash course in chanting from the Torah. Because the temple was Orthodox all three girls would have to wear long dresses with long sleeves. I, mistakenly, scheduled the shopping for these dresses right after we all received a series of needed shots. It seemed a good use of limited time to drive directly from the medical unit of the State Department to a good shopping area. Unfortunately, as the children tried on their clothes, their arms became increasingly sore and I felt increasingly guilty making them take clothes on and off until everyone had selected an appropriate wardrobe.

On one of our first Saturdays in Ethiopia, we decided to attend the synagogue where the bat mitzvah would take place. It was certainly not like any temple we had ever seen or imagined! It was in a building that had once been a mosque, but a very tiny mosque. My husband joined the men in a small room that served as the chapel. It was up one flight of rickety stairs. There were about fifteen men present and there wasn't room for many more. The girls and I were directed up another flight of those rickety stairs and we found ourselves in a tiny balcony. There were no other women present and we could understand why. We could barely hear the service and it was visible only through one small window. We took turns trying to see what was happening below. Although we attended the services quite often after that, there were seldom any women present except on special holidays. Even then, there were only a few women and they did not seem at all interested in seeing what the men were doing.

There were many Ethiopian Jews in the country but they lived far from Addis and had their own services. Only one Ethiopian Jew was part of this small congregation. The rest of the gentlemen were businessmen from Aden. They had been in Ethiopia for many years and had decided to stay when other foreigners left after the arrest of Haile Selassie.

As the time for our daughter's bat mitzvah neared, we became very nervous because the congregation changed the subject whenever my husband brought it up. If we could not discuss the arrangements, we obviously could not have a bat mitzvah. However, just one week before the special occasion, my husband, in desperation, managed to convince the leader of the congregation that we were serious about this event. This leader then offered to come to our home to see if Sheri could really recite the Torah. Since she had clearly studied hard and did an excellent job, he said he would keep his promise and allow her to enter the chapel and read from the Torah. But not before he asked, one more time, if people in America really did let girls participate in Jewish services. It was incredibly hard for him to imagine such a thing.

On the big day, my husband entered the synagogue as usual but Sheri could not join him. She was made to wait outside until her turn to chant. Her sisters and I stayed with her instead of going to the little balcony. We did not want to leave her alone and we felt we would have a better chance of hearing and seeing by peering in the door rather than through the little window. Every male member of the congregation was present, and the little balcony was crowded with women, some of whom had never come to services before. My husband told us that when Sheri came in the room, everyone fell so silent that he could hear the clock tick. Until then he had not realized the temple had had a clock.

My two other daughters and I had the opposite experience because a small boy in the courtyard chose the time of Sheri's reading to run his little car back and forth over the cobblestones.

Although we could hardly hear her, and could only see her back, I was filled with an overwhelming amount of motherly pride. We know it was the first bat mitzvah in that little temple and we are pretty sure it was also the last. But what a memorable experience for our family!

Since we knew that Orthodox Jews could not drive on Saturdays, we held the customary celebratory luncheon on Sunday. All the members of the temple attended the luncheon, as did many of our American and Ethiopian friends. We were later invited to dinners with this Jewish community and felt privileged to be welcomed. We recognized that they had made a huge concession for us. Sheri's cake had "Congratulations Sheri" written in English, Hebrew, and Amharic. That Sunday proved to be one of warmth and friendship among our different cultures.

Something Not to Write Home About

There are some things that you just don't include in letters to your mother. Being fired on is one of them. It happened while we were living in Addis Ababa. One morning while Princeton was in his office, I was at home ducking under windows listening to the sounds of bullets and louder sounds of unknown weapons outside.

When the shooting started, I ordered my two oldest daughters, 14-year-old Cindy and 12-year-old Sheri, into the hall in the center of the house, safely (I hoped) away from all windows and outside walls. I had also sent the cook, the houseboy, the laundress, several painters who had picked the wrong day to work in our residence, and the dog, to the crowded hall. The laundress had become hysterical and ran back and forth between the outside laundry room and the house. My youngest daughter, six-year-old Lori, was playing at a friend's home. I called the friend's nanny and told her not to bring Lori home until I phoned again to say that it was safe. I had also called my husband to suggest he stay at work until I called him with a similar message.

My husband advised the American embassy of the shooting and they, naturally, became concerned for my family's welfare and the welfare of another American family across the street from us. That family, it turned out, was hiding under beds as several bullets whizzed into their home. The ambassador joined my husband in his office and they kept calling me for updates.

I kept answering the phone, frightened at leaving the relative safety of the hall and angry at being asked to do so. By now, however, the entire embassy was concerned, not only about the American families near the shooting, but also about the cause of the incident and what the implications might be for the already strained relationship between Ethiopia and the United States.

Since the other family was apparently in more danger than ours, the ambassador wanted as much information as I could give him. Actually, I was not very helpful. I had not led the type of life that would teach me to identify various weapons by the sound they make. I don't even watch movies that might teach me something about artillery. (For the next two years of our stay in Ethiopia, I was teased relentlessly about the fact that when asked if there were mortars being used, I said I didn't know but something was making a "loud boom boom noise.")

Our cook kept going to the window to see if he could tell what was happening, and I kept yelling at him, "Get away from the window! What do you see?"

Which was about the message coming to me from the embassy: "Stay safe, but keep us informed."

When the shooting finally stopped, Lori and my husband came home. We looked out of the window and were shocked to see the remains of the house kitty corner from ours. It had huge holes in it, because the army had, after an exchange with other weapons, indeed fired mortars.

We also noticed seven bullet holes in our window and curtains! It was the same window through which our cook had tried to figure out what was happening. This large self-confident man was taken aback when he realized the danger he had escaped.

Although none of us could know it at the time, this violence had nothing to do with American dealings with the government in Addis. It was simply a matter of two American families being in the wrong place at the wrong time.

It took several days for us to hear the full account behind this frightening incident. The man who started it was an Italian who had owned a factory in precommunist Ethiopia. When the government took over his business, he applied to return to Italy. Instead of granting his request, the government forced him to continue managing what had been his plant. He was given impossible goals and was not allowed to criticize his workers. His position became intolerable.

On the morning of the shoot-out, he put his wife and dog in a cab and told them to go to the airport and leave the country. He went to his office and killed his secretary and the factory manager. He returned to his home, which he had previously stocked with great numbers of weapons and ammunition. When two policemen arrived to arrest him, he shot one of them in the foot and they immediately sent out an alarm. Soon, an entire company of soldiers surrounded the house and started firing. He fired back. For over two hours bullets flew in every direction. Finally, with the mortar attack, the man was hit and killed.

Will I mention this incident in my weekly letter to my mom? Absolutely not!!!

Trouble with the Law

The only one who really terrified me was the tall, thin stereotype of a cruel policeman; something about him suggested an eagerness to inflict pain. He never smiled and he held his rifle rigidly at his side, business end up. What probably made him seem especially scary was the twitch in his left cheek and the tight set of his mouth. I felt that any little annoyance or simple misunderstanding could end in tragedy. I did wonder just how long a person could keep himself looking so sinister when his captives were merely five unarmed and obviously very frightened female schoolteachers.

Our interrogator didn't seem as menacing as the tall silent one. His words were harsh, but he had a bemused expression that implied that he found our predicament more humorous than serious. I suppose the scariest part of the situation was the knowledge that we were guilty and everyone in the room knew it.

All I wanted was to be out of that Ethiopian police station. How could a first-grade teacher like me end up in such a predicament? My life revolved, innocently, around my husband, my own three children, and my first-grade students who were, at this moment, being taught by a substitute following, I hoped, my lesson plans.

A few months after our arrival in Ethiopia, the communist government had kicked out all American military personnel and most of the American embassy staff. They were given only four days to pack up and get on a plane. Because AID meant American dollars, we were allowed to stay.

The situation we teachers now found ourselves in started decades earlier when Haile Selassie ruled Ethiopia. He wanted to have an American school in Addis Ababa so the American Community School was established. He encouraged the school to teach an American curriculum using American textbooks and American personnel. After his death, the communist government that took over Ethiopia by force had an altogether different attitude toward the school.

The harassment of the American school began even before the majority of Americans were sent home. The Ethiopian government told the Ethiopian employees to arrive at their school assignments late and then not do their jobs. They were not to attend staff meetings. The school administration was informed that no Ethiopian employee could be reprimanded or fired. The most recent demand was that Ethiopians, not Americans, should hold all the teaching positions. The school administration was told that teachers needed work permits, and those would only be granted if it could be proven that no Ethiopian could do the job. It became evident that the communist definition of being qualified to teach an American curriculum from American texts had something to do with political connections and nothing to do with qualifications such as teacher training or experience, or even an ability to read English.

That's how, on what had started as a normal school morning, I found myself in this hostile Ethiopian police station.

As soon as my little first graders were settled at their desks, the school superintendent, an American, had appeared with a substitute teacher for my class and asked me to come to his office. There, he explained to four other teachers and me the latest communist attempt to take over the school. All teachers were to appear at police headquarters immediately. The superintendent had come up with a plan. He would send only those teachers who had diplomatic immunity, in the hope that we would be protected by this immunity. Each of the five of us in the room had a spouse in the American official community. (Although many Americans object when a foreign diplomat is allowed to return to his country when we suspect that he has broken one of our laws, this immunity can—literally—be a lifesaver for an American justly or unjustly held in a nonfriendly country.)

We five agreed, with some misgivings, to represent all the teachers. An Ethiopian school employee was sent along to drive the school van and to interpret. This young, wiry, somewhat sullen man was surely in the most danger, since death for appearing to side with the Americans was not out of the question. Nevertheless, he didn't hesitate to accompany us. The only instruction the superintendent gave us before he wished us good luck was that, no matter what happened, we shouldn't admit we were doing anything wrong.

At the police station, we were questioned repeatedly about our work permits. We were put in a windowless room barely large enough for us. Fortunately we were allowed to stay together. They brought in six dilapidated metal chairs whose plastic seats looked as if they might have once been red. The room was not dirty or messy, just joyless, with bare gray walls and several gray metal desks and file cabinets. There was a slightly unpleasant odor of male sweat. We could see a large opening into a wide hall where men in ill-fitting uniforms, some with weapons and some without, constantly walked by, often stopping to stare in at the surely unusual sight of a group of American women. Sometimes, one or two of these men would come in and talk to our guards. We assumed they were asking questions and/or giving orders about what should be done with us.

I can still picture Dorothy Walker, one of the high school social studies teachers who had both of my older girls in her classes, perched primly on one of the broken-down chairs. Her students were impressed that she always looked pert and pretty. She not only had a purse and shoes to match each of her outfits, she also had matching pens. Her color that day was Kelly green and I knew that there must be a green pen in the tiny green purse she held tightly on her lap. Her green high-heeled shoes barely reached the floor.

The school counselor, Jean Sutherland, seated to Dorothy's right, was a take-charge person who managed to speak for us in her thoughtful calm way. (Jean was to be severely tested when her husband, Tom Sutherland, was held captive in Lebanon for six-and-a-half years.) Next to Dorothy was Carol Roth, the other so-cial studies teacher, who also taught English as a second language. She was a friend with whom I enjoyed playing tennis.

The three of them sat across from Molly Sherman, the high school English/business teacher, and me. I could not see Molly, without turning my head, as her chair had been set next to but slightly behind mine. I wondered if she was able to control her habit of biting her nails when under stress.

I wondered if I looked calm, which was how I felt at first, but my concern turned to apprehension, and then to just plain fear as the situation dragged on and on. When questioned, we admitted, orally, that we were working at the school and we admitted that we did not have permits. We refused to admit that we were breaking the law (which I can understand was frustrating to our interrogators). But that was what we had been told to say.

After over two hours of this stalemate, each teacher was presented with a paper, written in the Ethiopian Amharic language, and told where to sign. We insisted that we wouldn't sign something we couldn't read. Our guards became agitated and angrily stated that the paper was only a transcript of what we had confessed. They told us that our refusal obviously meant that we thought they were lying about the content of the papers and this was an insult. We continued to refuse, but I was beginning to understand how people can be made to confess to crimes they haven't committed.

The policeman who at first had seemed to see the humor in the situation was now irritated and his manner hardened and became threatening. He clearly did not appreciate our lack of trust in his promise that if we signed the papers we would be allowed to leave with no further consequences. He informed us that we would remain where we were until we did sign. So, there we were: five teachers, an interpreter, and our interrogator and armed guard. None of us had any idea of what to do next.

After what seemed like the proverbial eternity but was probably less than another hour, we were presented with a new alternative. They told us we could leave if we handed over our passports and Ethiopian ID cards. Since it was against the law to be without this identification, I had visions of the five of us walking outside without our documents (especially our diplomatic passports) and immediately being arrested for that crime. Without much discussion, we refused this ploy and went back to just sitting there, with the police and the guard growing even angrier.

At this point, I wanted to talk to my husband and to tell him where I was. I wanted him to check on our three daughters who attended the school where I should have been teaching on this beautiful sunny day. I wanted him to get me out of this place. In a small, frightened voice I asked the interpreter to see if they might let me use the phone. Much to my surprise, after much Amharic discussion with men who we assumed were supervisors, I was granted permission. I called Princeton and told him of our plight. He was appropriately shocked and informed the American consul general, the person responsible for Americans in difficulty. In an amazingly short time he arrived at the police station. Not long afterwards, all of us very relieved captives were sitting in an American embassy van.

Never before had one of these beat-up, uncomfortable, old, faded-blue vans actually looked beautiful. Except for the interpreter, we were too shaken to go back to school so we went to the Embassy to get some reassuring hugs. I'm sure the Ethiopians were as relieved as the Americans that a face-saving solution had been found: recognizing our diplomatic immunity. Why the school superintendent had not thought to notify the American embassy when his teachers did not return after a reasonable time is a question I still can't answer. Perhaps he felt that connecting the school to the embassy would actually increase the Ethiopians' resentment toward the school.

The next day, I returned to work and the normal stress produced by twenty-six little six-year-old children didn't seem so stressful at all. When the superintendent was again asked to send all the teachers for interrogation, he stated that we had been mistreated and he would thus not comply with any such requests. Whew!!

Although the harassment continued in other ways and, eventually, the American school became an international school, we were able to continue giving the children the good education they deserved. My class of kids from fourteen different countries was a happy oasis where I could forget for a while the turmoil in the country.

What a Doghouse!

There were so many bomb threats at the American Community School that we became used to teaching to the sound of footsteps on the roof, as employees searched for (and fortunately never found) bombs. Ethiopia was definitely a hardship post; but as often happens at such posts, the ties of friendship were strengthened by helping and understanding each other. Our family actually lived in fear that the U.S. government would send the dependents out of the country.

After we had been there two years and it came time for our home leave, we planned to spend our holiday in Washington, D.C., and in California. We promised the girls that we would stop in a Kenyan game park on the way back to Ethiopia and, to compensate for some of the hardships, to look into the possibility of owning our own horse for the remaining two years of our posting.

In Washington, we had arranged to stay at the home of friends who were out of town for the summer. On the first Monday after we arrived home, Princeton dutifully headed off to work at AID headquarters in a rented car and the girls and I took a bus to the nearest mall to start our shopping. We needed to buy clothes and shoes for the next two years.

After work, Princeton met us at the mall and we all went to have dinner. After showing him our purchases, we asked him how his day had been. After much hesitation, he finally confessed that he had news for us. We were not going back to Ethiopia; the State Department had a job for him in Washington.

My daughters and I looked at him in disbelief, as each of us tried to digest the news and its impact on our lives. There were immediate practical considerations, such as the fact that we had just signed a new two-year lease with the tenants in our home and had no place to live. Also, except for the clothes in our suitcases, all our things, plus our dog, were either overseas or in storage.

Would the government pay to let us go back to Addis and pack out? My husband had already tried to arrange the round trip but the answer had been "No." He was told that friends would have to pack our things and ship our dog.

But, what about saying good-bye? There is always some sadness in the farewell parties, packing out, saying good-byes, and leaving an overseas posting, forever, but it can be really heart-wrenching when leaving a hardship post. And yet, the government saw no importance in our need to say good-bye to American, Ethiopian, and other foreign friends.

And what about our plans? I had signed a contract and was looking forward to another two years of teaching first grade. Our oldest daughter, Cindy, had made close friends while completing 9th and 10th grades. She was looking forward to finishing high school in the same small, friendly overseas school. Now she started to cry at the thought of not seeing her friends again and having to start her junior year in a huge school where she would not know anyone. (Her unhappiness was, indeed, to last through her high school graduation.) Our middle daughter, Sheri, on the other hand, was delighted at the prospect of going to a large American high school. Our youngest daughter, Lori, going into third grade, was not that concerned about where she would go to school. She made friends easily. However, all the worries of her parents, the unhappiness of her oldest sister, and the knowledge that we had no place to live were disquieting for her.

We could not register the girls for school in Washington until we had an address. So before we left to spend the next few weeks with my family in California, we had to find a place to live. We did approach our tenants only to discover that the man had recently had a heart attack and could not be asked to move. Eventually, we found a Foreign Service family going overseas for two years and rented their home for about the same rent we were charging. We contacted AID employees in Ethiopia and arranged to have our things packed out and our dog *not* shipped until we returned from California.

We returned to D.C. from our California trip expecting to move into our newly rented house. We checked into a motel and my husband went to his new job and said he would arrange to have our furniture delivered to the rented house. That turned out to be easier said than done. The storage facility had us listed as being in Ethiopia and was not about to deliver our furniture anywhere. Although Princeton could show them that he was obviously not out of the country, they had paperwork stating that he was, and they seemed determined to continue to store our furniture for another two years. We had to pay motel bills for several weeks while the government went through the process of writing a letter that would allow us to retrieve our furniture.

Naturally, our dog (appropriately named Gypsy) arrived during this time. She couldn't stay in the motel with us so we moved her into our completely empty rented house. At least twice a day, one or more of us would visit to take her for a walk, feed her, and play with her. Then she was left to enjoy the world's largest doghouse. It took us a long time to convince our new neighbors that we were not completely bizarre!

Nigeria 1986-1989

Bonding

When Princeton was notified of the opportunity to become ambassador to Nigeria, our youngest daughter Lori was about to enter her senior year in high school. We decided not to pull her away from that special year. So I stayed behind with her to let her graduate with her class and continue in all the activities with which she was engaged.

It was a particularly harsh winter that year in Washington. After a bad storm our power went out for several days. Each night, Lori and I would make a fire, and huddle close to it wrapped in sweaters and blankets to keep us warm. We were proud of ourselves for taking care of all the things that we usually left to Princeton. And on those cold nights together, we became closer than ever before.

Later, while in college, Lori would visit us in Nigeria each summer. Once after spending a weekend at one of Nigeria's newest Hilton hotels with friends, the group of them found their bills all confused and incorrect. Lori took charge. Only four foot nine, Lori, standing on a suitcase in front of the desk, went through each and every bill with the clerk and negotiated until all the charges were correct. When Princeton heard the story, he suggested Lori become a lawyer. She hadn't thought of it before. She would go on to law school and a highly successful career in government. But I think the spark of leadership in her may have developed that year when she and I held our world together all by ourselves. I know it bonded us in a way we had not before.

Ten Black Sedans

With sirens blaring, the line of black bulletproof Lincolns and Cadillacs forced its way through the crowded streets of Lagos. In some of the cars, earnest U.S. Secret Service agents with weapons and walkie-talkies eyed everyone in sight. Other security people on motorcycles zoomed back and forth among the cars, causing great antagonism from pedestrians and drivers who had been stopped to let the Americans through. U.S. Secretary of State George Shultz was visiting for one day.

I was in the sixth car watching the process with great anxiety. Several days earlier I had been given a 45-page book stating, to the minute, where I was to be and when. I had had to memorize which car I would ride in and where I would sit for the ten various rides we were scheduled to take. I had a list of times that I had to be in my seat for each trip. For example: En route to the Embassy, I would be in Car Six with my husband. Later, I would be in Car Two, after the lead car of the Secret Service, with Mrs. Shultz on the way to a clinic she was to visit. Then, it was back to Car Eight for another event. If I were late, even by a minute, the motorcade would go on without me.

In advance of the visit, I had been instructed to walk and count the steps that Mrs. Shultz would take at the clinic, which, as a former nurse, she was interested in visiting. Some of the program had to be eliminated because there were more steps than someone in Washington thought Mrs. Shultz could manage. She was disappointed when told of the cuts.

So this is how it went. Following the hospital visit, Car Two took us to a school where we met our husbands, and Secretary Shultz said a few words. Then it was a dash to Car Eight, where I rode with the embassy's political officer, while Mrs. Shultz rode with her husband. My husband rode with a senior person on Secretary Shultz's staff.

Our motorcade then proceeded to the Embassy, where Mrs. Shultz stood by the secretary's side, as she always did when he addressed American Foreign Service officers. (The Shultzes seemed determined to set an example of how spouses should support their husbands and how husbands should respond to their wives.)

Service49

As all Foreign Service families know, as exciting as such visits are, there is a sigh of relief at the end, as we watch the visitors' plane depart for their next stop.

Durbar

We Americans pride ourselves on our celebrations: New Year's Eve, the Fourth of July, weddings, birthdays, bar mitzvahs, and any other occasion we can turn into an excuse to party. We love music, fireworks, dancing, special foods, being together, and, in some cases, just showing off what we can afford (or want people to think we can afford).

But, in my opinion, there is nothing we do in the United States to compare to the vitality, color, and lavishness of a Nigerian Durbar. These ceremonies are held all over northern Nigeria, but by far the most spectacular ones are held in cities like Kano and Katsina. Watching it in Katsina was the experience of a lifetime.

The Emir of Katsina sat on his horse in front of the grandstand, dressed from turban to toes in sparkling white. Only his hands and eyes were visible. Several other similarly attired leaders of the region surrounded him. The crowds in the grandstand behind him were all male Muslims, plus several male diplomats and a few diplomatic wives who were willing to be at an all-male event in order not to miss the thrill of extravaganza.

At the far end of the huge arena, probably the size of five or six football fields, was a group of ten to twenty horsemen in brilliant colors and flowing robes—their horses even more lavishly outfitted than they, with blankets and decorated saddles, as well as jewels and feathers in their manes and tails. On the long dusty path leading up to the arena were similar groups waiting for their turn to be the center of attention.

When it was time for the program to begin, the emir lifted up his staff and the horses came at him at a full gallop. They were not allowed to stop until he lowered his staff, which, for those of us sitting in the honored seats right behind him, wasn't soon enough. After stopping up short and paying their respects to the emir, this group galloped away while the next group started toward us. For me, watching the retreating group was the most delightful part as their costumes billowed behind them in a most dramatic fashion.

This display lasted for several hours as group after group of handsome men had their turn to demonstrate their horsemanship skills and show off their wealth by the number of riders in the group and the grandeur with which they and their horses were dressed.

When the show was over, I was all set to pay the price, as I was seated for the 3 o'clock lunch between two of the gentlemen dressed from head to toe in white. I knew that these Muslims were not allowed to shake hands with women, and I felt that they must be most uncomfortable and unhappy to be seated next to the only woman at the table. I felt for sure they would both ignore me and spend the long meal talking to the person on the other side of me.

But, looks can be deceiving. One of the men had recently returned to Nigeria after receiving his MBA from Harvard and beginning a promising business career. His father, one of the chieftains in the area, had died and he was called back to take up the position. Though it would change his life and bring him back into the traditional demands of religion and constituency, he felt it his duty. Given his background, he was fully at ease with me and we had a wonderful conversation. There was much to learn beyond the color and ceremony of this celebration.

Kids

One of the ways I coped with my "ambassador's wife" life was to work. In Nigeria, I was very fortunate to be able to teach in the American school. I taught first grade and my time spent in the classroom with my little six-year-olds are some of my warmest memories of my diplomatic life. One of my little students was the daughter of the man who managed the Nigerian 7UP business.

One day, one of the other children was celebrating his birthday at school. His mother brought the usual cake and ice cream, plus a Coke for each child. The mother and I were busily going around the room opening the drinks when the young lady whose father managed 7UP came shyly to me with her open bottle of Coke. I was desperately trying to think of how to comfort her about all the Coke in the classroom and where I could get her something else to drink.

I needn't have worried. She simply smiled at me and announced: "I hate Coke, but I love to drink it." And so she did.

. . . and Angels

First-grade students make the most delightful companions, but they can cause a teacher stress even when they are being very, very good.

This story took place on a very average school day when we were studying the seasons. I was explaining and showing pictures of trees that had lost their leaves. I then showed an evergreen tree and started to explain the difference between the two kinds of trees.

At this point, a little girl raised her hand and looked so excited that I called on her immediately. (I was actually pleased to see her enthusiasm, because she was not one of my brighter students and she seldom participated in class discussions. Sitting here at my computer all these years later I can still see the sparkle in her green eyes that day.) She happily announced that she knew why those trees did not lose their leaves. She gravely went on to tell the story of an angel who fell to earth and was kept from hurting herself by a tree that held out its leaves for her. The angel rewarded the tree by ensuring that it would not lose its leaves in winter.

I thought a bit about her explanation and decided that the other children would learn their science facts soon enough. For today, I would let them believe in this angel. How could I have done otherwise and deflated the excitement of the little angel in my class?

Justice

Most of us loved the experience of living in this vibrant, colorful, and dynamic, if admittedly corrupt, country. The Nigerian people were a lot of fun, and those working in American homes and businesses and the school were hard working and loyal. Petty theft—usually of things not used—was rarely mentioned.

We teachers did not at first notice the slow disappearance of films and videos from the school library. We were, after all, practiced in improvising when something was not available, when the electricity went out, no water came out of the tap, or the phones were dead. So how much could we be surprised when the film we wanted to show our students was not in the library?

Eventually, however, a few teachers became suspicious when more and more requested films were unavailable. So an inventory was made and it was discovered that thirty or more films were missing.

One of the Nigerian school employees decided to set a trap. Unbeknownst to the school staff, he took it upon himself to sleep in the library. He was soon rewarded. One night, he watched in amazement as a coat hanger was lowered from the transom above the door and the lock was opened from the inside. The thief carefully opened the door and turned on the light. He was immediately recognized as a trusted fellow Nigerian school employee. He ran away, the self-appointed detective called the police, and the thief was soon in jail.

After some time, the school staff became concerned when no trial date was set and our petty thief started to deteriorate in his cell. He was not abused in any way, but he was not being fed properly or allowed to exercise or given medical attention. Efforts to withdraw the charges or force a trial date met with no success. We started bringing food and blankets and medicine to the man, but we were too late.

His death cast a lasting pall on the teachers and staff at the American school. Surely, this was one punishment that did not fit the crime!

Chieftaincy Ceremony

In early 1988 in Nigeria, we were very excited to be invited to attend the three-day chieftaincy ceremony of an American friend, Natalie. She was receiving the honor of becoming a white female chief in a small village near Ibadan because of the work she had done there to improve the lives of the women. She had contributed to the construction of a workplace for the women to produce a popular yam-like product. Childcare and health education were provided at the place.

We left Lagos very early on a Friday morning and drove to Ibadan, where we joined a sort of caravan of people and continued on to the little village over bumpy, dusty paths that were almost roads. After parking the cars and buses, we were escorted to the location of the ceremony by people playing instruments, mostly "talking drums." Our escorts walked backwards and drummed right in our faces. As they kept this up, we were expected to "spray" them, which meant we had to put paper money on their foreheads. The money stuck because it was hot and the drummers were sweating. The money was removed so quickly that I guess it wouldn't have mattered much if it hadn't stuck.

The whole scene was so unreal: hot and crowded and noisy and ever so colorful. It was just plain fun! Princeton caught a pickpocket with his hand in Princeton's pocket. The man said "sorry" and disappeared into the crowd. We were moved around to various seats of honor (most people had to stand). In the end, Natalie was whisked away and no one really got to see the actual ceremony. She returned with a sort of branch in her hair and a coral necklace. She was now a chief. Lunch for about five hundred people was served (very slowly) with a lot more drumming.

Lodging had been found for us in a home in Ibadan, and we were provided with outfits to wear to the dinner that evening. Princeton and I wore clothes made of the same material and when we arrived at dinner found about forty other people also dressed in clothes of the same material. We were thus designated as part of Natalie's tribe. Again, there were hundreds of people at the dinner. Afterwards we learned to dance to the beat of those drums.

There was such a happy atmosphere that even our driver came and joined the dancing. He was quite good, but said that Princeton and I looked funny doing Nigerian dancing. I'm sure he was right. We even looked funny just standing in our loose-fitting, one-piece, stiff African-material clothes and hats. Tall and elegant Natalie looked perfect.

The next day, our tribe of forty was taken to Oshogbo, the cultural center of western Nigeria. Our host was a man named Twin Seven Seven, because his mother had had seven sets of twins and all the babies had died except him. A colorful and flamboyant artist and musician, he was at one time a politician. He had been involved in a terrible auto accident that left him with a bad limp (which didn't seem to slow him down a bit). He believed that the "accident" was an assassination attempt and so dropped out of politics.

He took us for an "audience" with the Oba of the area (a sort of royal person who greets you from a throne and has men with swords standing on either side of him). We paid our respects.

We would return to Oshogbo many times. We would visit the sacred park, where fantastic statues from the Yoruba religion had been constructed by a mysterious woman who had come from Austria, converted to the Yoruba religion, and rose to become a high priestess. We also went often to the home of Twin Seven Seven to hear his band, to admire his art (even to purchase one of his paintings), and to enjoy the warmth of his and many other Nigerians' friendship.

South Africa 1992-1995

Townships

The white minority in South Africa established townships (really artificially created communities) when they decided that it would be better if white and black and colored people lived separately at some distance from each other. As might be expected, the whites decided that they should be the ones to live in the cities and the coloreds and blacks should move elsewhere. So black homes were plowed into oblivion and their owners transported to barren land miles away.

Some families were put into very small, poorly built houses for which they had to pay rent. Others were expected to be happy with the structures they could erect themselves out of scrap materials on the land they were given. They were not allowed to have stores in their townships: everything had to be purchased from white storekeepers in the city.

Their children were not taught math and science, because they would not be allowed jobs that required those skills. They were to be grateful for buses to ride two or three hours a day in order to get to work and buy their groceries. Those lucky enough to have some work had to get up long before dawn to start the two-hour trip to fix breakfast for some white family in a home with heat and air-conditioning and running water, and a garage that was larger and in better shape than their shanty dwellings.

The black townships were huge and crowded with shacks springing up everywhere on treeless land, with few paved streets or sidewalks. Every time I visited a township, I could not help but wonder how people managed to survive—especially the men. The women often had jobs in the cities or were busy with the children and the cooking and the laundry. The children were able to play with homemade balls and old tires and stray dogs, or attend schools—even if the schools were ill-equipped and usually lacked supplies or indoor plumbing and, sometimes, were located under a tree. But, the men, just hanging around, maybe gambling with each other, and often drinking, were the saddest sight.

Most of the violence that was inevitable in the face of the draconian treatment of the majority of the population was hidden and contained within these townships. I never witnessed the abuse of women, the rape of children, the killing for a jacket, a hat, or a slice of bread. However, I did believe those stories that were told to me as, feeling depressed and helpless, I viewed the barren landscape, the shanties crowded together with their cardboard windows, rusting tin roofs, unpaved paths, and lack of adequate electricity or plumbing.

When the violence spilled out into the cities and suburbs, then everyone heard about it. Both whites and blacks could be murdered in a car-jacking, even if there was no need to kill, the car readily given up. Homeowners, shopkeepers, and pedestrians were grabbed and felt the knife while losing their property.

Should we wonder at the violence? Or should we look at the hastily thrown together one-room shacks, with their roofs that let in the rain and trapped the African heat, and picture what we might be capable of if we had to raise our children there? During the final years of apartheid, before the election of Nelson Mandela in 1994, the violence spilled out in increasingly massive protests, in spite of the cruel consequences the police dished out to the protesters. But the protesters may just as cruelly have punished those fellow township residents who refused to protest. If, to feed the family, a person went to his or her job on a day the township had called for a strike, it was not uncommon for activists to douse a tire in gasoline, throw it around the guilty neck, and set it on fire. There was no mercy as the person tried to explain why it was necessary to work that day; no mercy as the person screamed, then became a silent, burnt body.

A culture of violence had been bred, and it is a legacy that even a free South Africa continues to confront.

Mandela, My Hero

I first met Nelson Mandela when Princeton and I had only been in South Africa a few months—a turbulent few months. Mandela had been released from prison two years earlier. There was progress toward a majority rule government, and most South Africans, "black," "white," and "colored," were passionate about avoiding civil war. But the political reality was still a dizzying roller coaster ride. One day some seemingly insurmountable difference would suddenly be at least partially resolved. But then the next day the newspapers would be full of graphic descriptions of riots following a township killing. After each horrific event, all sides would blame the others and call off negotiations. The outcome of this march toward a democratic government was still unknown.

It was during these unsettled times that Princeton and I arrived in South Africa. We had high hopes and some fears of what his tenure as the American ambassador would bring. The African National Congress (ANC), Mandela's political party, did not harbor friendly feelings toward the United States, which had come to the anti-apartheid movement rather late and, in the ANC's opinion, was still not giving it enough support. The white-ruled South African government, for its part, did not trust us because it felt we were *too* aligned with the forces intent on replacing it.

By April 1993, conditions were not much improved. But, fortunately, there were men like Nelson Mandela who were able to convince most black South Africans to give nonviolence a bit longer to prove itself. Another was Chris Hani, who, like Mandela, had great charisma and popularity. He was a dynamic young man with the ability to control the youth vigilantes, who were becoming dangerous.

That's how things stood one day as we sat with the DCM and his wife in our living room in Cape Town. We were waiting to hear that a visiting U.S. congressional delegation had boarded their bus and were on their way to see the Cape Flats townships. We were all exhausted from ensuring that the delegation was having a safe, informative visit, which we hoped would send them back to the United States with more determination to aid the South African struggle. Today the group had a full program planned, leaving the four of us free. This Sunday seemed made for hiking on the famous Table Mountain. Nature had blessed this part of the country by surrounding it with two oceans and then adding several magnificent mountain ranges and forests.

It was relaxing to be in the presence of good friends with whom I could just be myself, sip my coffee, wear my old jeans, sink into a soft chair, anticipate the planned hike, and wait for the call that would signal the end of our responsibilities for the visiting Americans. We felt we had earned this rare chance to be out of the spotlight and just enjoy ourselves the way other people did.

When the phone rang, I eagerly reached for my backpack with no premonition of what was to come. Once I realized, from Princeton's side of the conversation, that something had gone wrong, my disappointment was overwhelming. But the horror of what had happened quickly put all thoughts of beautiful, peaceful Table Mountain out of my head. Chris Hani had been assassinated.

We knew immediately that the country had lost the very man, after Mandela, most capable of keeping order in the townships. We had lived through the American riots after the assassination of Martin Luther King and feared for the future of South Africa's hope for a peaceful transition.

Soon we learned of the ANC's plans to have two memorial services for Chris Hani. One would be for the diplomatic community and would take place in Johannesburg, the major business city in the country. The other would take place a day earlier on a football field in Soweto, a teeming black township of five million people. Princeton decided to attend both of these services. I objected on the grounds that the one in Soweto was sure to be dangerous; there had already been several reports of violence around the country. He insisted that he would be safe—so I insisted that if it was not dangerous, I would go along. I thought that argument might keep him safely at home. But my plan backfired and, along with my husband, I found myself being driven to the football field, accompanied by an armed American security employee. There was one bulletproof vest, my husband's size, hanging in the car.

As we drove toward the stadium, I became increasingly fearful listening to the angry shouts of the young men walking to the service. Fires had been set, and rocks were being thrown at the steel military and police vehicles that were visible all along the road.

Although we arrived early, the stadium was already packed. People were standing everywhere in order to see, including on the rooftops of the small buildings around it.

So it was that we found ourselves the only diplomats and, indeed, the only white faces that I could see, at the entrance of a football field crowded with 10,000 agitated ANC and communist mourners.

Once inside the stadium, Princeton and I were taken over by four huge men wearing red shirts with "Communist Party" printed in large black letters on the front and back. Trying to smile and not show our nervousness in the midst of the chaos and noise, we explained who we were and were greatly relieved when we realized that these tough-looking young men had become our self-appointed bodyguards. We sincerely hoped that they were up to the job. Very unceremoniously, two of these hefty men held Princeton's arms down by his sides, lifted him off the ground, and literally carried him through the crowds. The two others did the same for me. Thus they transported us safely across the length of the stadium, to the platform where they thought we belonged.

During this time my heart rate was going through the roof, and I felt we had been stupid to come to this event. In our protected white world we could not comprehend the feelings of the masses around us. Later, much later, we were able to joke that, were we to have appeared on American TV surrounded by men in communist party shirts, our stay in South Africa might have ended quite abruptly. Politically incorrect or not, they kept us from any threat of harm and, looking over the angry faces of the crowd chanting anti-everything slogans, we were grateful for their protection.

We sat through increasingly irate speeches and became ever more concerned about where Hani's assassination would take the crowd and where it would take the country. When Nelson Mandela finally arrived on the scene, even he seemed in danger of losing control of the crowd; he was booed several times when he spoke out against taking revenge. In the end, to our great relief, he did manage to quiet the people, partly by stressing the fact that it was, after all, a white woman who had taken down the license plate number of the car of Chris Hani's assassin. After his speech, Mandela was told of the American ambassador's presence, and we were informed that he was coming over to greet Princeton.

I was (and am) used to standing in the background while my spouse conducts business at receptions and dinner parties and all manner of social occasions. I am rather shy, and especially uncomfortable around celebrities. So it was with relief that I stepped back as a world hero stepped up to speak to my husband, the American ambassador who, by attending the memorial service, was expressing his support of Mandela's goals for South Africa. Mandela noticed me in the background and our eyes met. Although he did not know me, he seemed to size up the situation immediately. I could feel him thinking: "Awww, poor thing, she's shy." And then, in spite of the tension we could still feel in the stadium—in spite of the concern he must have had about what he needed to say and do in the next few days to keep the black population's anger from erupting into a violence that would kill his dreams of a peaceful change of government—over he marched to give me a hug.

Nelson Mandela is loved and respected worldwide for his charisma, courage, and the fact that he is a strong leader whose integrity is legendary. But as that encounter demonstrated, it is his kindness and sensitivity to others that have made him *my* hero.

(The *Foreign Service Journal* previously published this essay in May 2004. Reprinted with permission.)

News Event

For those of us praying for a peaceful end to the apartheid era that had caused such suffering in South Africa, the news that came gave us hope that a disastrous civil war could be avoided. It also gave credence to theories that fate is often the invisible yet leading player in human history.

Archbishop Desmond Tutu best expressed the joy of this news event when he said, "I am just over the moon. This new dawn was going to be overcast, but now the sun is shining."

Zulu Chief Mangosuthu Buthelezi, the principal actor in the episode, said, "South Africa may well have been saved from disastrous consequences of unimaginable proportions."

These consequences would have been caused by none other than Buthelezi himself and would likely have thrown the whole country into a civil war.

The problem, just a week before South Africa's long-awaited first democratic election, was that Buthelezi was planning to boycott those elections and was asking his seven million subjects to do the same. Buthelezi had been one of the most important anti-apartheid leaders while Nelson Mandela was in prison and had actually been a loud voice demanding Mandela's release. But when Mandela was finally freed, the two leaders each felt the other was not giving him appropriate respect, and their relationship fell into one of mistrust. As Mandela's popularity grew, Buthelezi felt more and more that he would not have a proper place in the future government of the nation. He wanted to ensure a leadership role for himself before he would commit to the election. The dispute was more than between the two men, however. Their respective parties had already become engaged in violent conflict that had taken 3,000 lives.

Foreign diplomats in South Africa—as well as world leaders who flew into the country—tried one method after another to talk, bribe, threaten, and plead with all of South Africa's leaders to find some compromise that would bring Buthelezi into the election. Less than ten days before the election, at the request of the two parties, the United States sent Henry Kissinger and Great Britain sent Lord Carrington to mediate the situation.

Buthelezi made delaying the elections a condition to talks, but Mandela would not accept that condition. So Kissinger and Carrington returned to their countries with no progress to report, and Buthelezi boarded a plane to return to Natal, the part of South Africa where he lived and ruled.

On the ground at the Lanseria airport was another mediator who had not drawn much attention; in fact, it is not clear who invited him to the negotiations. As the plane flew off, he felt he had missed his chance. He was a Kenyan named Washington Okumu and he had befriended Buthelezi. They shared a deep Christian faith, and this is where fate came to South Africa's aid.

Buthelezi's plane developed mechanical problems and had to return to the airport. Buthelezi described this turn of events.

"It was as if God had prevented me from leaving, and I was there like Jonah brought back from the whale."

Okumu was able to use that feeling to convince Buthelezi that he must think of the lives that would be lost in a civil war and that he must be willing to make some compromises to save those lives. Okumu went on to meet with Mandela and de Klerk and then asked Buthelezi to join them. With just a few largely cosmetic changes to the interim constitution, the deal was made.

So, just one week before the election, the country set out to print nine million gummed Buthelezi labels to stick on the bottom of the ballots. This was a very small price to pay for the peaceful election that took that beautiful country from apartheid to democracy.

Very Important Visitors—Handle with Care

"I can't believe you've got me doing this," Princeton grumbled as he shuffled down the hall carrying his pajamas and toothbrush.

"Oh yeah, baby," I answered, "and you've got to go back for your razor and some clothes because you'll be using the guest bathroom to shower in the morning."

"Oh, come on, now you're getting ridiculous." His mild grumbling turned into major irritation.

"No, I'm not. If we are going to go through with this, we might as well do it right and shower and everything in the guest rooms."

Nelson Mandela was to be inaugurated president of South Africa and the whole American diplomatic community was scrambling to get ready for V.I.P. visits from Hillary Clinton, Vice-President Al Gore, Tipper Gore, and a constantly growing and already seemingly endless list of members of Congress, business leaders, and celebrities who were to attend the event.

After years of working desperately hard on the huge issues that could have stood in the way of a peaceful transfer of power from F. W. de Klerk's white minority National Party to Nelson Mandela's African National Congress Party, we were reduced to worrying about the innumerable details that had to be taken care of to make certain that each of those Americans coming to Mandela's inauguration would feel that they were treated as the most important person at the event.

We diplomats had to learn to keep egos happy. As the wife of the American ambassador, I was responsible for the comfort of Hillary Clinton and the Gores, all three of whom would be staying with us at the ambassador's residence.

Although, at the time, I had no way of knowing that our careful preparations would not be sufficient for a pleasant stay, I did have a premonition that our residence could not be turned into a palace fit for a king—or even for a vice president and his wife and the first lady of our country.

It was Kathy, a friend of mine from the embassy, who told me that before the secretary of state visited Kenya, the ambassador and his wife had checked into the very rooms at the Kenya Hilton that the secretary would occupy just to make sure that he would be comfortable. Kathy had mentioned this precaution taken in Kenya without suggesting anything. But I had learned the hard way that I had to read between the lines when people spoke to me, because no one seemed able to treat me normally enough to actually come out and tell me something. (I had stopped asking people to call me Helen since the response, even from Kathy, was always "Yes, Mrs. Lyman.")

So, Princeton and I were testing our own guest rooms for comfort.

Our residence, though it had a great deal of space for entertaining indoors and outside in its incredibly beautiful gardens, only had three bedrooms. While each of these was more than adequate for Princeton and me, they were not anything to write home about. Each room was large enough, with a desk and lots of closet and bureau and book space, but all the furniture was standard government issue, bought in huge lots to keep the price down. Now, trying to see it through the eyes of dignitaries, it seemed plain and shabby.

"First thing tomorrow we'd better tell the staff why we're sleeping in this room with the twin beds instead of in our queen-sized bed. They'll have the whole diplomatic community buzzing by noon if we forget."

All went well that night and morning after we slept and showered and dressed in what would be Hillary's room. But, when we went through the same procedure in the Gores' room and I was happily enjoying a wonderful, long, hot shower, my husband knocked on the shower door and tried to make himself heard over the sound of the spray.

"Hey, hurry that up, I can't see a thing in this fogged-up mirror."

"Well, turn on the vent, for heaven's sake."

"I can't find a switch, and I don't see a vent."

Three hours later a crew of four had installed a vent in case Al Gore might want to shave while Tipper showered.

Kathy and I, during those same three hours, were totally engrossed in the serious business of selecting the towels that would be placed in the V.I.P. bathrooms. Should we buy the white ones with pink roses, or the maroon-and-grey striped ones, or the solid blue ones, or the blue-and-white striped ones? And what about pillows and sheets and soaps and candles and snacks for the rooms?

After the shopping trip came the staff meeting with the advance team for the advance team. I had also been asked to find a hairdresser.

My lifesaver of a hairdresser, Rosalie, was actually looking forward to doing Hillary's hair and thought she could talk her friend, Judy, who did both hair and make-up, to come with her to take care of Tipper. She even gave me the name of someone to be on call to give Al a massage if his back went out.

Of course, all the experienced American diplomats at post in South Africa expected an advance team to come out to get us ready (in the way Washington thought we should be ready) for our high-level government visitors. But we had never heard of an advance team coming out to get us ready for an advance team. When we heard this was going to happen, we knew we were in for some hard times.

Advance teams are necessary, of course, and there are usually some helpful people who quietly and tactfully let you know important facts, such as that your whole home will have to be set up for a communications system that would allow Vice-President Gore to take over as president in the event that something unfortunate were to happen to President Clinton. We would need to supply towels and such for the Secret Service, special assistants, and the doctor, who would all be sleeping in our home. Staff and secret service people would also be standing guard outside the house.

"Don't worry, all the extra people are used to sleeping in halls and sharing bathrooms," the leader of the second advance team assured us. He and three of his men walked a group of seven of us embassy types to the grassy area where we would hold the reception we had been told to host after the inauguration.

"Now, this is where we'll put the rope and we'll hold all the guests behind it," he continued, while he pointed out the entire width of the lawn from the side of the tennis court to the fence at the end of our property. "The platform for the guests of honor will be about 16 feet in front of the rope and you'll need a microphone there. The vice-president and the ambassador will finish their working dinner with high-level embassy staff at 7:30 P.M. and arrive at the start of the line to start shaking hands at 7:43. Someone will tell the ladies when to leave the residence so they will arrive just as the men start greeting people. Mrs. Lyman, you will walk along the rope shaking hands but not stop to talk or make introductions. Mrs. Clinton and Mrs. Gore will follow you."

At this point, he showed me how to shake a hand in such a way that I could move down the line quickly and avoid any conversation. "That's called 'grip and grin.'"

"Now, Mr. Ambassador, you will stand here and speak for three minutes and introduce the vice-president and Mrs. Clinton. Each of them has prepared a statement. Then you will introduce Tipper, who has not yet decided if she wishes to speak, but will let you know. There will be a chalked "X" for each of you to stand on. Mrs. Ambassador, when you reach the platform you will step back so the other two ladies can cross in front of you and then you will move up to your "X" next to Tipper Gore. Mr. Ambassador, you will step back after you introduce each speaker and they will move to your spot to speak."

He was not done. "The port-a-potty will be next to that little gazebo, and the line will go backwards toward the back gate."

"Wait a minute," I said. "We have two guest bathrooms on the main floor of the house and have never needed additional facilities for our functions."

"No one will be allowed in the house for any reason."

"Even though the guests will have to show their invitations and go through a metal detector?"

"Right"

"Oh."

And so the days of preparation flew by. I tried to keep the peace between our house staff, the embassy personnel working on the events that would take place in our residence, and both the helpful and not-so-helpful folks from Washington. Princeton was having an even harder time negotiating between the U.S. government and the South African government, which was unbelievably busy planning the inauguration and providing the logistics and security necessary to host thousands of people and the heads or almost-heads of most of the world's countries.

"The South Africans want regular South African citizens to be able to share in the day's events, and they want to impress world leaders with their ability to provide first-class hospitality," Princeton confided in me. "Each country has been given a certain number of seats at the breakfast and at the inauguration; each has been allowed three cars in the procession that will go from the breakfast to the inauguration. South Africa will provide landing instructions as close to the desired landing time as possible. South Africans will greet each arriving delegation and provide transportation as needed. And South Africa will provide a program the night before the big event.

"Washington, of course, is not happy with this and will not comply with any of these rules," my husband complained, "and I am caught in the middle. The other countries are generally satisfied, but I have already negotiated for five times the number of allotted seats and permission to land extra planes at special areas for security. We are the only ones who didn't accept South African limousines, but flew in our own on huge jets. While many other countries have played important roles in assisting South Africa, our government seemed to feel that only the United States has done that and so we should get special treatment."

So Princeton spent the time before and even during the events of the big day seeing what extras he could obtain from the South Africans and trying to convince the Americans not to ask for more. It made working on the change of South African government seem easy by comparison.

Princeton and I had to explain to a very dignified elderly South African official that the American plan for our visitors' arrival was a bit unusual. "Hillary Clinton and the Gores want to descend from a plane together so they can be greeted together," Princeton explained, and that made sense. "The only problem is that they will not be arriving on the same plane."

What we didn't tell the South African was why. It seemed that the White House did not want anyone in the American delegation to feel slighted. So, since we were sending two planeloads of people, Hillary would fly with one group and the Gores would fly with the other group—everyone would fly on a White House plane.

"So if you will be so kind, sir, could you board Hillary's plane with my wife and me and we will greet her, while the rest of the delegation disembarks and goes by bus to their hotel. We will, if it doesn't inconvenience you, wait until the second plane arrives and then, somehow, sneak Hillary onto it so she can walk down the plane stairs with the Gores." (Never mind that the airport would be crawling with reporters and assorted officials ready to greet various delegations, including ours.)

The South African official was too much of a gentleman to react. He simply said, "That will be fine."

Of course, our delegation arrived in the rain. The second hitch came while we were waiting for the first flight to land. All of a sudden we were told that Mrs. Clinton's plane had already landed at the opposite end of the field. They were sorry we had been waiting, for an hour, at the wrong spot. So, with the elderly South African running along beside us in the rain, we managed to be by the plane, diplomatic smiles in place, when the passengers, minus Hillary, came down the plane stairs to shake our hands.

An hour later, when the Gores arrived, there was, fortunately, enough confusion that we did manage to sneak Hillary into the back of their plane unnoticed, get in line, and greet her with the proper enthusiasm.

That night, we all attended a beautifully moving program honoring many of the people who had fought so hard for a democratic South Africa. Instead of enjoying the program, Princeton spent his time on a cell phone. The problem now was that Mrs. de Klerk had invited Hillary, Tipper, and me to breakfast the following morning. This made for some understandable logistical changes so that I would ride with the two ladies and Princeton with the vice-president. But, the Secret Service said that they would then need an additional six cars to provide the proper security since we were not all going to exactly the same place.

I watched Princeton's face as he thoughtfully listened to his cell phone and then spoke softly.

"The Secret Service has already told me that they can't allow it unless they can use another six cars, so please tell Mrs. de Klerk that the ladies are truly sorry, but they simply can't come to breakfast."

He then whispered to me, "The South Africans are arguing that since the breakfast you ladies would attend is on the way and only two minutes before the main breakfast we men will attend, the Americans surely can't need another six cars. They have already grudgingly allowed us six instead of the three cars that every other country has agreed to."

But, then came the call stating that Mrs. de Klerk was already depressed and upset about stepping down as first lady and considered this a sign that she was now considered a nobody. In the end, we got our twelve cars and went to the breakfast.

My next challenge was at the second breakfast, where we caught up with the men. I had been taken to this venue several days earlier and shown a suite of rooms to which I could take Mrs. Clinton, Mrs. Gore, and their group to freshen up and relax before the inauguration. Princeton would stay with Al Gore and introduce him to the appropriate dignitaries, and I would stay with the women and provide introductions and information as needed. The aides around the women, however, made it so obvious that they thought I was hanging around them hoping to meet dignitaries that I found Princeton and begged him to let me stop sticking with them.

He said, "Sorry, but you have to do this."

Reluctantly, I returned but stayed in the background until I saw them sneak out and escape down a hall. "I bet they're looking for the bathroom," I said to myself and literally ran after them while they were telling me to stop following. I finally got one aide to listen to me. "I know where you can all relax in a suite of rooms to which I have a key." They followed me up two flights of stairs and down several hallways and, by some miracle, I didn't get lost. As I had been directed, I stayed with them and now was simply ignored instead of snubbed.

We faced yet another challenge at the inauguration itself. Two young Gore staffers took our seats. "You'll have to sit in the diplomats' section" one of them had the nerve to tell my husband, the ambassador.

"These are their seats," said Al Gore, knowing, as we all did, that there was no diplomats' section. The staff members sheepishly got up and gave us the seats.

Dinner with Mrs. Clinton and Mrs. Gore went well; they seemed to enjoy the simple meal that their staffs had ordered for them. My cook had fixed a light but tasty pineapple sauce for the chicken, mixed just a few raisins into the rice, cooked the beans to perfection with a few honeyed almonds, and served the salad with a selection of dressings. Her dinner rolls were her specialty and were served hot out of the oven. Although the cook was told not to fix a dessert, everyone ate her tiramisu with only a murmur about the calories.

The conversation was pleasant enough as we chatted about the day's events. I did manage to ask Hillary, "Is it a relief to get away from the reporters in the U.S.?"

"Yes," she answered honestly, "they are being horrid to Bill right now, and they won't leave me alone; but we asked them to please stay away from Chelsea and they have been wonderful with her. I am so grateful about that I don't complain about the rest."

The reception that evening was in honor of all our visitors, and the entire American community had been invited. It was so odd to walk along the rope that held back the crowd and shake hands with people who were my friends and coworkers, even though I knew they had wormed their way to the front to shake hands with Hillary and Tipper, and not me. Still, it was comforting to see their familiar faces and encouraging smiles.

When the speeches started I went to my "X" at the front of the platform. (A few days later, when we saw the photos of the event, Princeton and I and our friends got some good laughs. I was only in the first shot: it had taken Jesse Jackson only a minute to maneuver himself in front of me. By the third photo I was entirely invisible as others managed to get themselves in full view of the audience and the camera.)

When the speeches were over and the ropes came down for the VIPs to mingle with the crowd, I thought I could relax. But Princeton found me and whispered, "You have got to get poor Maya Angelou out of that long line for the port-a-potty."

"But will the Secret Service let me take her in the house?"

"Of course, they'll recognize her and you are wearing that pin they gave you."

I approached Maya and asked, "Would you rather come in our

house for a bit? It's right over there."

"How sweet of you dear, that would be lovely, are you sure it's OK?"

"It's my house, how can they keep us out?"

Quite easily, as it turned out. Now I had just made things worse for her, and she would end up at the end of the line again. Fortunately, Princeton had been watching us and, when he realized what was happening, found the head of the Secret Service detail and convinced him that Maya Angelou and I weren't much of a threat.

A few days after the whole visit was over and our guests had left, I found time to get my hair done. I greeted my hairdresser, "You can't imagine how happy I am to just come in here and collapse for a couple of hours—if I can remember how to relax." I was also anxious to hear how her experience with our visitors had gone.

"Well, it was fine, Mrs. Lyman. Judy and I showed up at 5:30 a.m. not at 6:00 because we were so nervous that we might be late. It was a good thing, because the guards took over a half hour to check every curler and lipstick and dryer and bottle we had with us. They frisked us, and the dogs had to sniff us and everything else. They didn't even kid around when we tried to lighten things up a bit. What a serious bunch. We explained that we had so much stuff with us because we didn't know what their hair was like or how they would want to wear it. We got so nervous because we had been told they wanted their hair done around 6:00 a.m. and it was 6:20 before we got in. Still, we just sat downstairs until after 7:00. Then I had to stand outside Mrs. Clinton's room and listen to her yell at an aide or someone until I finally got called in around 7:30."

"Oh, Rosalie, I'm so sorry. Did she at least apologize and pay you well?"

She hesitated before answering, and that was not like her at all. "She was fine with me, really, don't worry. I knew she was in a snit so I didn't say much, which, you know, is not like me."

It occurred to me that my question about pay had been avoided, so I asked her again if she'd been paid. I lied that the money would come from the embassy not my pocket if she hadn't been. It turned out neither she nor her friend had been paid. As I handed her the money, I asked:

"Rosalie, do you know why Mrs. Clinton was in such a foul

mood?"

"Well, from what I heard before I was called in, she was furious about two things. First, her aide had packed the wrong suit for her to wear to the inauguration, and second, she had been awake all night because there was some little refrigerator in the bedroom and it kept going on and off all night and made a horrible noise every time it switched from one to the other. I guess someone must have thought it a nice idea to stick it in there after you and your husband had tested out the room. Did they even tell you about it?"

I could only mumble, "No, they didn't."

Grandchild

My oldest daughter Cindy and her five- and three-year-old daughters came to visit us in South Africa. We took them to a resort where they saw elephants and giraffes and many varieties of deer. They stayed in our embassy residence, which had lovely gardens and a swimming pool and staff that catered to their every whim. They rode in a lift to the top of Table Mountain. They spent time at a beach where they enjoyed walking and swimming in the water with penguins. They crossed the ocean in a jet plane.

When asked if she enjoyed the visit, the three-year-old said: "Yes, because Gramma gave me the best banana."

The Representative of a Superpower

One of the things Nelson Mandela had in common with my husband is that he made his own phone calls (instead of having a secretary get someone on the line and then make that person wait while the person making the call is found). When at their desks (or in this case, in bed), they also answered their own phones.

At 7:20 a.m. on Saturday, February 14, 1995, the phone in our bedroom rang and my groggy husband answered it with a simple "hello." The voice at the other end slowly explained, "My name is Nelson Mandela," to which my husband answered, "Good morning, Mr. President."

President Mandela continued: "I wonder if it would be possible to speak to the American ambassador."

The reply was: "Speaking, Mr. President."

President Mandela then said: "I'm sorry, Princeton, you didn't sound like the representative of a superpower."

Off to See the Queen

Even a sometime rebel like me can't really say "no" to an invitation from the Queen of England, even though we were in Cape Town and the reception was scheduled to be held in Durban, a two-hour flight away. But, dutifully, we set off on a Friday afternoon packed for hot and normally humid Durban. This time, it was cold and rainy when our plane landed.

Arriving punctually at 8:30 P.M. at the harbor, we discovered the dock was filled with people who seemed to be delighted to be standing there in the rain. Having an invitation did allow us to get out of the rain and enter a very large warehouse-style room, which eventually held the 300 or so "B" list. (We were the ones not invited to the dinner, but invited to the reception.) There were some puddles on the floor and life rafts and such hanging from the ceiling, but everyone was in a great mood. We all remarked to each other how glad we were to see the much-needed rain. We could not have cared less about our hairdos. It was fun to see who else was there and watch them look around to see who else was there. (Princeton was delighted to conduct some urgent business with some people he had been unable to pin down during the week.) It was also fun to note what people were wearing. The range was from those who obviously thought, "I'm going aboard a ship on a cold and rainy night," to those who thought, "I'm going aboard the queen's yacht." So we had the casual wear and the long elegant gowns and everything in between.

After a half hour in the warehouse, we noted a general movement to a door and joined the queue. It moved slowly past British marines making sure we had our invitations. A group pushed in between Princeton and me, so I was detained until he noticed my absence and assured the marines that I was the Mrs. on his invitation. Through the door we got our first glimpse of the *Britannia*—she is an awesome sight. Once on board, we stood in line again to go past some more marines checking our invitations. No one thought much about that, and we chatted casually as we moved toward the corner where we were being checked again.

At the corner, a marine simply said, "We ask that the gentleman goes first for protocol reasons," and he handed our invitation to another marine who introduced us to the queen and Prince Philip before we knew what was happening.

Checking with people later, we found everyone, like us, thought it was a security check line and didn't realize it was a reception line. The royal couple did do it right. They both looked very regal—he very tall and straight and she with a diamond tiara and long gown. She offered a white-gloved hand for a royal handshake. They do look at you and smile as you mumble that it is a pleasure to meet them. In person, the queen is much prettier, softer, warmer, and more gracious than she appears on television or in the papers.

In the reception rooms, we were constantly offered wine and a variety of soft drinks and lots of little snack things. We had had dinner but could have filled up quite well on the "snacks" that kept coming around. The queen mingled with the guests but, alas, did not join our group. Someone who had been lucky enough to be in a group that included the queen said that the conversation had been mostly about cricket. There was a famous (to those who know about these men) cricket player and a famous rugby player in the crowd.

Just before 10:00 P.M., we were asked to go on deck. The rain obligingly let up just at that time. For those, like us, who enjoy marching bands and pomp, the next half hour was a delightful experience as the Queen's Band performed with great marching band music in great style. Although they had a limited space in which to maneuver, they managed to come up with a magnificent array of formations to march for a half hour in the same spot. This was the official retreat, although the queen had a full day on Saturday and the *Britannia* was staying on for ten more days. Flags were lowered, anthems played, and great applause for whenever President Mandela or the queen waved.

After that, we watched the "A" group depart. A "who's who" of the new South Africa, one by one, walked down the gangplank and got into the middle of three cars (presumably the back and front cars were full of bodyguards). Off would go that set of cars, and the next set of three appeared. Then it was our turn to leave, and we felt that it had been a grand evening indeed. "Fit for a queen," one might say.

The next morning, while waiting for our plane, we spotted Walter Sisulu, one of the great patriots of the South African liberation movement, and went to pay our respects. I got a kiss on the cheek, which was the perfect ending for a special visit.

Farewell Lunch with Mandela

When President Nelson Mandela learned that Princeton's tour as ambassador was coming to an end and we would be leaving South Africa to go back to Washington, he called and offered to host a private lunch for the two of us. We were thrilled that we would have this private time with Mandela instead of seeing him at one more reception with a hundred people standing around juggling food and drinks and trying to make conversation.

When the day of the luncheon arrived, it was decided that Princeton would bring the huge picture of Mandela and Clinton that was America's inauguration gift. (Never mind that the South Africans had requested a pen that would sign Mandela's name automatically.) Having lost the argument with Washington that we should comply with the country's wishes, we now had to present the new president of South Africa with this huge picture that would probably end up in some storage room.

My husband's driver brought the picture to our residence, and we discovered that there was no way the ambassador, the political officer, and I could fit in the car with the picture for the drive from Pretoria to Johannesburg. It was decided, since Princeton was the honored guest, that he should ride in his chauffeur-driven car, with the picture, to be sure to arrive on time. The political officer volunteered to drive me in her old car, hoping that we might also make it in time.

Since it was a hot African day and the car had no air-conditioning, we had to choose between being extremely sweaty when we arrived at Mandela's home or open the car windows and be extremely windblown. We arrived sweaty *and* windblown and with wrinkled dresses. But, we arrived on time.

Mandela himself opened the door for us, and we settled in his living room, which, like the rest of his house, was just like any ordinary home. The room had plain wallpaper, and the sofa and chairs were a bit worn but large and comfortable. Princeton presented Mandela with the huge picture of himself and Clinton, and Mandela was able to look politely pleased, though we knew he must have been disappointed. His home was so warm and friendly with various mementos and art tastefully displayed—what on earth was he going to do with this huge picture?

After chatting for about twenty minutes, Mandela suggested we move to the dining room for lunch, where his granddaughter would serve us. The dining room was furnished in the same comfortable style as the living room and contained a sturdy, plain, wooden table and comfortable dining room chairs. I was asked to sit next to the president, Princeton across from him, and the political officer across from me.

I remember the food as being quite tasty but nothing fancy or elaborate. Mandela's granddaughter, about twenty, was pleasant as she served and took away plates. Had she also fixed the food? I didn't ask.

After lunch, the coffee was served while we were still sitting at the table. Mandela offered me sugar and cream for my coffee. I declined and told him that I drank it black.

He said, "Well, you should take sugar and cream. Don't you know that we African men like our women to be a little round?"

When we finished our coffee it was obviously time to leave. President Mandela was his usual gracious and gentle self as he bid us good-bye, thanked us for our work to help make the transition happen peacefully, and said he would miss us.

I was floating on my own special cloud. This day seemed like a reward for any hardships imposed by a diplomatic life style.

Leaving Post

What to Do When an Ambassador's Tour Is Over

1. Inform Washington of a convenient time of departure.
2. Control anxiety as the time nears and Washington has made no response.
3. Understand that the time of your desired departure will pass before you receive an answer.
4. Receive an answer confirming an inconvenient time for departure.
5. Request "orders" (the paperwork necessary to arrange for plane tickets, packers, etc.).

6. Inform embassy and consulate staffs, residence staff, other diplomatic missions, host country officials. (This step is a necessary formality in spite of the fact that the rumor machine will have done the job before you finish reading your "orders.")

7. Set the date the packers will come.

8. Set the dates for the farewell parties: the embassy, the consulates, your residence, your friends, other diplomatic missions, etc.

9. Avoid having people invited to too many farewell parties, without offending anyone by asking them not to throw such a party.

10. Arrange future employment for your residence staff.

11. Prepare farewell gifts.

12. Sort your belongings into piles of what you will pack in your suitcase, what will be sent to you by air (within the small limit set by the government), and what will take three months to come by sea freight.

13. Make time to watch the packers carefully so all your belongings are put in the correct boxes and no embassy goods are packed by mistake.

14. Make arrangements for visits to friends, vacation stops, or meetings you wish to attend en route to your home or next assignment.

15. Purchase tickets and reserve hotel rooms for the trip home.

16. If you have a residence in a second city in the host country, repeat steps 7,10,11,12, and 13 in the second city.

On the occasion of our scheduled departure from South Africa I had finally gotten it all right and the above steps were carried out with only minor difficulties. But, as usual, no matter how well I follow all the rules, something is sure to happen to add an extra challenge to the situation. This time was no exception.

Everything had gone well the week before at our residence in Pretoria. Today, after our second pack-out, we had just watched the crates with all our Cape Town belongings hammered shut and driven off our driveway.

The whole experience had been exhausting, so we settled down in our cozy den and asked our butler to bring us drinks while we relaxed. We had just been served when the phone rang and the butler came back to tell us the call was for Princeton. He was gone a very long time and I was just about to follow him to see if there was bad news when he entered the room with a most dejected expression.

"You won't believe this," he said. "That was Washington calling to tell us we can't leave. The vice-president is coming for a visit."

How to Prepare for a Vice-Presidential Visit after Your Belongings Are Packed, You Have Airline Tickets and Hotel Reservations Out of the Country, and You Have Had about 1,000 Farewell Parties

1. To avoid embarrassment, pay for your own tickets and leave the country temporarily.
2. Explain the situation to employees, friends, and diplomats from other countries, who, by now, tend not to be surprised at America's ways of doing things.
3. Arrive back in country in time to make proper arrangements for the visit of the vice president and his wife.
4. Arrange for lodgings and events to be scheduled at venues that have not had their belongings shipped out of the country.
5. Purchase new tickets to depart from post directly home.

Planning a Day with Tipper

1. Let her advance team make arrangements with employee staff.
2. Do not ask questions when told that you will ride in a car three cars behind her. (She prefers to be with people she knows already and the second car is for security). In the heat and in high heels, somehow catch up to her in time to make introductions at each stop.
3. Do not ask questions when you notice that three different events have been scheduled for the same time at the end of the day because Tipper has not decided which of these events she prefers.

4. Smile politely all day.
5. When Tipper makes a rest stop, get back into your car when told that you may not do the same.
6. When Tipper intervenes and allows you to make a rest stop too, hurry because the car will not wait for you if Tipper is ready before you are.
7. Love the South Africans because, at every stop, they wait for you to catch up and show their friendship to you.

Photo Gallery

My parents Adolf and Sidi Ermann.
They fled Nazi Germany in 1934 and
made their home in San Francisco.

With my daughter Lori,
1986. A year of bonding.

Celebrating our daughter Sheri's Bat Mitzvah
in Ethiopia, 1976. The cake had congratulations
written in English, Hebrew, and Amharic.

Our daughter Tova and her husband Chanina at their
very Orthodox Jewish wedding, Jerusalem 1987.

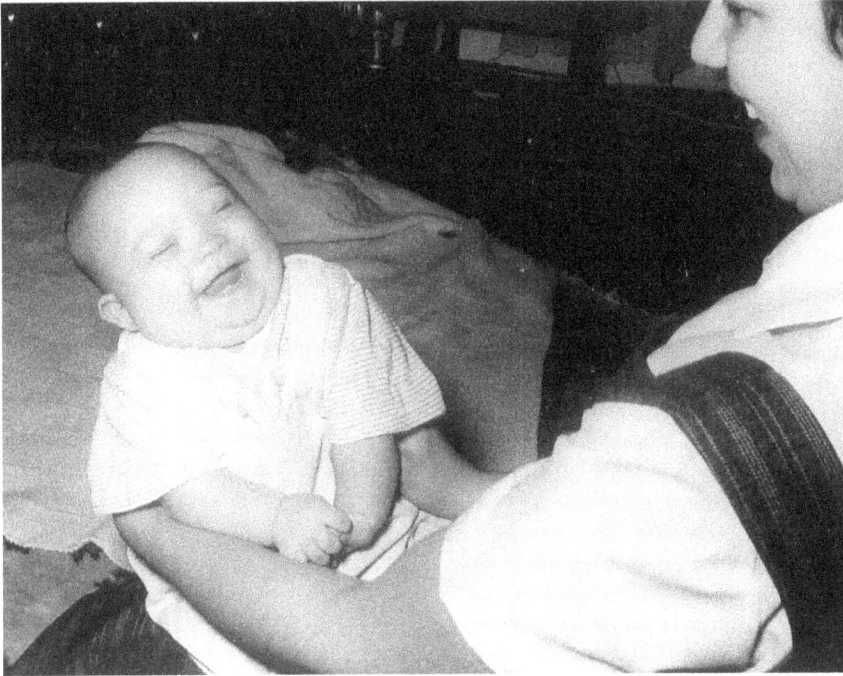

Our always smiling son Kevin, 1961. He would pass away a few months later, leaving a hole in my heart.

My angels in first grade at the American School in Lagos, Nigeria, 1988.

Lunching in Beijing 1990. Teaching computer software for the State Department made me a world traveler.

Teaching State Department employees in our small office in the State Department, 1991.

The beauty of South Africa has always stayed with me. Looking across the plains, 1993.

Albertina and Walter Sisulu, giants of the liberation struggle, always greeted me with such warmth and affection, even when I was escorting Washington VIPs! Johannesburg, 1994.

To be part of history in South Africa was an honor and a thrill. Helen and Princeton at our residence in South Africa, 1994.

Our farewell lunch with Nelson Mandela, 1995. He is my hero.

Opening of the U.S.–South Africa Binational Commission in 1994. We hosted the commission co-chairs, U.S. Vice President Al Gore and South Africa Deputy President Thabo Mbeki.

My beloved brother Don, 2007. He was always there for me.

Post-Foreign Service

United States

State Department Spouse's Role

For forty years, I worked very hard at being the proper diplomat's wife, but it was always a struggle and I never felt that I got it quite right. This time, in 1998, there was no doubt that I had done something that didn't meet the expectations of the State Department.

I was asked to be a member of a panel of ambassadors' wives who would speak to and answer questions from a group of twenty-one women preparing to accompany their ambassadorial husbands overseas. The ladies organizing the panel had had trouble finding ambassadors' wives willing to participate so seemed enthusiastic to find me, willing and working in the same building where the panels were held, with a boss who thought it a good opportunity for me to put in a little plug for his computer training program. These sessions for wives occurred only every two or three months, when a large enough group of newly appointed ambassadors were being trained. I had looked forward to participating, but it took me a while to realize that I was not going to be asked to come back a second time.

The four of us on the panel sat at a long wooden table facing the women who were taking advantage of this opportunity to find out more about their future roles. Looking around, I saw that I, like everyone else in the room, was in appropriate diplomatic dress, designed to look well without attracting attention: a well-tailored suit; matching heels and purse; small but real jewelry; light on the make-up; and beauty-parlor hair. I had not spilled food or coffee on myself and didn't think I had heaped too much lunch on my plate.

The first ambassador's wife on the panel had given good and needed advice on the immediate steps to take when realizing that one is about to go overseas as the spouse of the senior American diplomat. She explained how to find information about the country that would be a temporary home and about the living conditions for Americans. How do you find out such essentials as an appropriate school? Can you buy toilet paper? What is the climate? Do people dress formally for diplomatic functions?

The second wife spoke about equally important issues such as deciding which of your things to pack for the trip, which to send by air freight, which by sea, and which to put in storage.

The third spouse explained what needed to be done after arriving at the new assignment. For example, how to select household staff, being careful not to offer greater benefits than other diplomats, because they would complain that they then had to pay more just to hire or keep employees. Even more important was not hiring someone away from another foreign or American family. She also discussed how to meet the foreign and American communities and such issues as asking for help from the American spouses at post. She mentioned that she kept a list of what she wore to functions so that she wouldn't wear the same outfit twice in a row to events where the same people would be present.

I was the last speaker and managed to find an entirely different subject. I told the story of my first experience as an ambassador's wife. Because my youngest daughter was a senior in high school when my husband went to Nigeria as the ambassador, I stayed behind in the United States for nine months so that my daughter could graduate with her friends. The ambassador preceding my husband had been a bachelor, so my husband kept the house staff and protocol assistant, who took care of the residence, shopped for and cooked his meals, and took care of all the details necessary for diplomatic functions, from the invitations to the after-dinner drinks.

When I arrived in Lagos, all that stopped, and I was asked to come up with menus, order flowers, shop, and so forth. I told everyone on the staff that they should just continue to do all these things as they had before I arrived—that was *their* job. *My* job was to attend functions outside our residence, be the hostess at functions in the residence, and teach first grade in the American school in Nigeria.

I used this story to make the point that wives could do their diplomatic duties and still have a life of their own. Because in Nigeria many events were stag, I had time to make my lesson plans in the evening. Also, because of the heat, school started early and was over by 1:30 P.M. So, if I needed to attend a function such as the American Women's Club annual fund-raising fashion show luncheon, I could get a substitute teacher for the last two hours of class. I was honorary president of the club, and they had their monthly meetings at our residence. If the meeting was a tea, I could attend, but if it was scheduled as a morning coffee, the women still held it in the residence, with my staff serving, but without me.

Another hint I gave was that, every evening, when my husband came home, he would go over the invitations he had received that day. I put on my calendar those events he said I should attend. I did not put down those he said I didn't need to attend and which would not be interesting anyway. I would make a decision about those that were not necessary but would be enjoyable for me.

Obviously, I did not give a presentation that pleased the organizers of the panel. I also did not get as many questions as the other wives. So, it seemed, once again, that I did not get it quite right.

1990: Teacher Woes

From my classroom for five-year-olds, I could hear increasingly loud sobbing from the room next door. The three-year-olds in that room were supposed to be napping and were under instructions from the school's tyrannical superintendent not to make a sound. Each day, the children were sent to the bathroom before they went to their cots, and no additional trips were allowed during naptime.

In the past, I had been severely reprimanded for leaving my class to check on a crying three-year-old. But, as the child's sobs grew louder and louder and I could hear no sound of someone coming to check on what the problem was, I asked my little five-year-olds to be really quiet while I went to check.

The little boy in the next room was crying too hard to tell me what was wrong so I guessed he needed to relieve himself. When

I asked, he nodded his head, so I carried him to the bathroom and told him to hurry. Soon, I heard footsteps on the staircase so I told him to run to his cot and close his eyes. He made it back just in time, and the superintendent could not figure out which three-year-old had committed a grave sin. As I expected, she then stormed into my classroom and demanded to know what we knew. I lied that I had no idea, and all the wonderful kids in my class backed me up.

Those five-year-olds were the reason I had put up with the impossible conditions in the nursery school for as long as I had. But, in the end, my love for them was not strong enough to keep me working in such a child- and teacher-abusive atmosphere.

The nursery school was in a house, and I had been given a small upstairs room as a classroom. My fifteen kindergartners were supposed to sit, the whole school day, on little wooden chairs around a wooden table and not make a sound. The superintendent was on the floor below ours and came stomping up the stairs if she heard the children's voices or the scraping of a chair. The main job of the school, I soon realized, was to have the children produce papers that could be sent home to assure parents that their children had learned to read and write and do math.

According to the superintendent, the problem with my teaching style was that I didn't hit the children when they weren't perfect. When I refused, she started leaving hitting sticks in my classroom. She told me there was one boy who obviously needed more discipline, and she had told his mother: "Mrs. Lyman could hit him all day and he wouldn't feel it." This was meant to lure me to use the stick.

Rules for the teachers required that school supplies be requested only from the superintendent. A used-up pencil had to be presented to her before a new one was issued. I had once committed the terrible crime of asking her husband for some construction paper for a project. She found me waiting for him outside the supply closet, and I am sure he received a more severe dressing down than I did.

My final day at the school started uneventfully. Then, the superintendent came to the class and said she had solved the problem of my not hitting. She told me that, after I had left school the day before, she had spanked one of the boys and told him she was doing this at my request because he had been loud in class.

When the children had gone home, I slammed every drawer and every door as I went in and out to put my stuff in my car.

Botswana 1992

Diamonds Are a Country's Best Friend

Through my job teaching the use of computers to State Department employees, I was fortunate to visit the small country of Botswana. This trip marked the first time I had ventured into a foreign country all by myself. It was a great place to start.

Because of its geographical location, Botswana is a hot and dusty country where it is hard to make things grow. The people were so warm and friendly and everything went so smoothly for me, I had to find out a little more about this place that I had never heard much about. It's amazing that one almost never hears about this small democratic country when people are discussing Africa. One reason could be that people only talk about countries in trouble. There is very little conversation about a country that is doing everything right.

An extremely simplified history of the country seems to indicate that there is justice in the world. Many of the Tswana people originally lived in the area now known as South Africa. They were a peaceful people pushed further and further out by the Zulu people until they were on hot and dusty land that no one else wanted. Although many Tswana still live in South Africa, those on the dusty land were given their own country and left alone. Justice came in the form of diamonds. The Tswana made the most of this discovery and now have a peaceful and prosperous democracy to call their own. When a drought hit, Botswana did not need any international help to feed the people.

Unfortunately, like so much of Southern Africa, Botswana has been hit hard by the AIDS virus. Fortunately, because Botswana's government quickly admitted the seriousness of the problem and was prepared to deal with it, a combination of donors, universities, drug companies, and foundations have come together to help Botswana meet this challenge. Botswana has become a model and a testing place for finding the best way to control this disease in that region of the world. I feel very hopeful that the Tswana, with this cooperation, will lead the way.

Botswana also has a most wonderful delta area, where tourists discover the wonder of game parks and are able to view the animals on islands reached by boats moved along by guides with long poles that they stick in the mud. Another feature of this small country is that nature sends it great thunder and lightning storms without any rain. At one point National Geographic asked if they could set up some scientific equipment on the roof of the American Embassy in order to study this lightning. The embassy agreed, and soon fancy equipment was installed. It is not difficult to imagine the reaction of Botswana's neighbors when they observed all this commotion, wondering what form of American spying might be underway.

Uganda 2005

The long flight out to Uganda was pleasant enough, and Princeton and I were happy to spend the daylong stopover in London with our good friends the Speizers. They fed us and took us sightseeing and, best of all, provided excellent company for the day. The purpose of our trip to Uganda was for Princeton to attend a Childreach (formerly Foster Parent's Plan) board meeting. It was being held in Uganda so the board could see what Plan Uganda was doing with the aid it was receiving. We also wanted to see gorillas.

During the trip from Entebbe airport to our hotel in Kampala (a little over an hour), Princeton and I had the same thought: "It's nice to be back in Africa." Uganda gets plenty of rain and the fields we drove by were green. We saw the whole range of living conditions. There were a few lovely homes, some squatter shacks, and mostly in-between dwellings—shabby and poor but not real poverty. Everywhere it was bustling with life: small shops selling everything, people getting a shave or haircut in the open, barefoot kids running everywhere, and their older sisters somehow walking gracefully to work in their stiletto heels in spite of the rocky, uneven, dirt paths. There were cows and goats and bicycles and men playing games (surely for money), and lots of homemade TV antennas sticking up, some from dilapidated shacks.

Our hotel/resort/convention center was quite nice. It had lovely grounds, a restaurant with good food, television, coffee, and bottled water in the rooms, and speedboats and horses available for rent. It did not have air-conditioning or an elevator to take us to our 4th floor room. We figured climbing the stairs was giving us good practice for tracking the gorillas, but couldn't figure out why the night air in our room was hot, while outside it was cool.

We had time to unpack and shower and go for a walk before our 4:00 o'clock briefing. Plan Uganda had worked very hard on the two-hour presentation, complete with PowerPoint and handouts, and had done an excellent job. Unfortunately, the room was warm and the Americans had missed a whole night's sleep and were jet lagged. So we all kept smiling and waking each other up and trying to look awake. We didn't fool the Ugandans, but they were very kind and polite. The briefing was followed by a reception and outdoor dinner with the American ambassador (a friend of ours), the AID director, and various other American employees in Uganda.

Breakfast the next morning was at 6:00, after which we left to visit projects in Tororo, 3-1/2 hours away. We saw the Plan headquarters but spent most of the day at their health clinic. The clinic dealt with all the usual problems but was known for the great job it was doing to help HIV/AIDS sufferers. We were unbelievably impressed by both the staff and the patients. Since the clinic doesn't have the latest drugs, the health care workers prepared the infected people and their families for their deaths. The staff does this with lots of counseling, helping people to help each other, having people make memory books for each of their children, and teaching them skills to earn a living in a way that is not as strenuous as the farming most of them do. The staff also counsel the children and teach them skills they will need if they become orphans. The infected people educate others in the community through song and dance and theater. Fortunately, they do have the drugs that can often stop the transmission from mother to child. The Plan board is now trying to get the community into a pilot program to receive the antiviral drugs. We also visited some of the shops and a sort of community loan association that the Plan had helped set up.

We spent the night at a hotel in Tororo and visited more sites the next morning. Then it was another 3-1/2 hours back to Kampala. There were board meetings in the late afternoon. When the spouses were offered shopping and sightseeing, we all elected to shower and rest instead. Dinner that night was delicious but in a restaurant over an hour away and with slow service, so it was another late night. Princeton spent all of the next day at board meetings. There were so many important decisions to be made about the best way to raise money, the most beneficial ways to use the money, and the relationship between the U.S. board and the international board.

While these weighty matters were thrashed out, I was fortunate to go, with three other spouses and one board member's 13-year-old son, to visit Chimpanzee Island. We took an hourlong bus ride to Lake Victoria and a wonderful hourlong speedboat ride on the beautiful lake to the island. The fishermen who used to make their home on the island had been relocated so that rescued chimpanzees could be brought there to live out their lives in a free forest setting. Since there is not enough food in the forest to sustain the number of chimps, they get fed four times a day. They are fed in an area where tourists may watch them, separated by a fence.

Chimps are intelligent, social animals and a lot of fun to watch. There was one baby in the group and several were ready to help Mommy care for him. They each have distinctive personalities. The "alpha male" is quite clever. When one of the young males shows signs of becoming large enough to challenge the leader, the leader starts treating the youngster as his favorite, making him his best friend. The younger chimp is happy to be number two in the community and even fights off other threatening males to keep the leader in power.

The next morning, twelve of us piled into a bus that would take us to the area where we could track the gorillas. Because the roads were bad and the bus didn't have four-wheel drive, it took us until 8:00 in the evening to make the journey. We didn't mind making pit stops behind the bushes, but it was hard to find bushes that were hidden from Ugandan homes. We did stop where we crossed the equator, where Princeton and I had our picture taken together, although each of us was in a different hemisphere.

Our tents were rather basic, and trying to organize ourselves in the dark was another challenge. But we had a delicious meal and were able to sleep well in our cots. We found our tent life to be a lot of fun. The man who took care of our tent was named George and he woke us up in the morning (at 5:45) with tea and biscuits. Then he brought us the first shower; and, when one of us had finished, he brought us the second shower. In the tent, we had a thermos of hot water and a pitcher of cold water so we could wash our hands. George also brought us a small light bulb and we found that a generator provided for this little bit of light. Just like kids, we read in bed by flashlight.

Groups visiting the gorillas are kept small, so only seven of us could track the first day. Princeton and I and three others were not in that group, so the five of us went instead into the forest with a wonderful guide who took us on a 4-1/2 hour hike to a waterfall. He got us huffing and puffing, although we stopped often to look at monkeys, birds, butterflies, and various views of the magnificent waterfall. Rainforests are good places.

That night at dinner, the seven who had tracked talked of the wonders of seeing the gorillas, but also filled us with some horror stories of the tracking. They described not being able to breathe, slipping and falling, losing sight of the guide, wanting to go back, cutting up their hands pushing thorns aside, etc., etc., etc. Two mountain climbers in the group said it was more strenuous than any climbing they had done. The stories were so appalling that I became convinced that I could not do it and felt I should drop out so as not to spoil the trip for others. Princeton convinced me to give it a try.

So, after a hearty breakfast, we set out at 7:30 while those who had told us the horror stories looked on with worried faces as we departed. By 8:15 our passports and permits had been checked, we had been issued walking sticks, and we had been presented with porters who would carry our lunch and water, cameras and insect repellent, and so forth. Then there was a lecture on the etiquette of watching gorillas. You couldn't do it if you had a cold or any contagious disease, and you couldn't make noise or talk out loud. If you had to cough you were to turn your back on the gorillas and cover your mouth with a tissue. The guides had the authority to send you back if you didn't behave.

Finally, we were on our way with two security men carrying rifles, two trackers to hack away the forest so we could pass through, a guide, four tourists, and our porters. After about fifteen minutes on a path, our guide said he knew a shortcut, so off we went into the jungles of Africa. As predicted, the trackers had to clear a narrow way with their machetes, and our porters had to help us find footing and pull us up steep places. We needed the porters, the walking sticks, and the gloves to protect our hands from thorns. We crossed the river several times, and I was one of the few who didn't slip off a rock and get wet feet.

After about an hour and a half of this, the whisper came down that there were signs of recent gorilla movement. We did see broken branches and such. After another fifteen minutes we stopped, and the porters gave us our cameras and took our walking sticks and said they could go no further with us. We now had to be very quiet and, sure enough, within about five minutes, we saw our first gorilla. Gorillas are beautiful, dignified, and gentle animals with soft brown intelligent eyes. They are huge, and when they stretch out an arm you do half expect to see a small lady in their hand. The hour we were allowed to spend with them was beyond description: they are awesome. Humans feel quite humble in their presence. They must be protected!

The Ugandans have, indeed, taken significant steps to keep their gorillas safe. The number in Bwindi has risen from 320 to 350. Since the young need their mother's care for five years, the females only have a baby every five years or so. No population explosions to help out here. But the community around the forest gets 20 percent of the proceeds from tourism, has many people employed by the reserve, and sells to the tourists. Therefore the community is now enthusiastic about guarding the gorillas and recently turned in one of their own who had killed a gorilla.

After our wonderful tracking experience, we arrived back in camp by 12:30. We were teased that it had been too easy and we hadn't earned our time with the gorillas. After a shower and a rest, we were ready for more and were told about a walk around the villages. This turned out to be another unforgettable adventure. We met "real" Ugandans and found conversation easy and relaxed. Those we met were quite friendly. It turned into a four-hour trip. We saw a small, family-owned, banana-wine-making plant. The owners still used their feet to stomp on the bananas but assured us that they first washed their feet thoroughly. Our path then led us to a traditional healer. He explained his herbs and herb teas to us, and our guide told us that this healer had cured many people, including our guide. The healer didn't charge unless he cured the patient. Trained by his father, he kept his ingredients secret (like a patent). His wife was a midwife.

Then we had a long hike (seemingly straight uphill) on a road we shared with a great variety of people and animals. At the top of a mountain, we came upon a pygmy community. They had been living on the road, working each day just for the food, until the government gave them some property and taught them how to build homes and grow food. The pygmies sang and danced for us, and we felt compelled to buy some of their handicrafts, which were actually quite nice. Their dancing was also impressive, and we were told they had won competitions. They had a guitar, and one person in our group played and sang for them. They enjoyed that.

The next day, we spent another thirteen hours on the bus, but we did stop for a picnic lunch at a lovely resort on a lake. The Bwindi adventure was well worth the twenty-six hours spent in hot buses on bumpy roads.

Our last day was to have been spent visiting another Plan project, but everything was closed because it was a national holiday. So we went shopping in the outdoor markets and in a fancy indoor mall. The atmosphere in the outdoor markets was surprisingly pleasant with no begging, no hard sells or sad stories, just a little friendly bargaining. The mall was totally modern, with one supermarket that sold anything in the world one might want to buy. (Where was that market when we were living in Nigeria and Ethiopia?!)

The next morning brought one last ride through the countryside, and then it was time to say farewell to Uganda. Neither Princeton nor I had been there before, but both of us would be happy to go back. Although I have written much too much, I have not been able to find the words to do justice to the dignified HIV/AIDS victims or to the awesome gorillas.

Note: Today the Ugandans in the Plan's HIV/AIDS program are receiving ARV treatment and no longer have to prepare for death. Helen was so happy to hear that, but did not have time to update the essay. –PL

United States 2003

A Loss

I can't think of a name for what I lost, I'm not even sure how to describe it. I just know I miss it and don't think I will ever find it again. It is a sort of warm feeling I used to get when non-Americans showed their good feelings toward us as Americans. I think we felt it as a nation immediately after 9/11. Around the world people found ways of letting us know that they shared our grief and wished us well.

One strong memory of my feeling that warmth dates back to my days in Ethiopia. The Ethiopian government had recently been taken over by communists, and relations with the United States declined rapidly. So, it probably should not have come as such a shock when the word came that all military personnel and their families had four days to pack up and leave the country. Most of our embassy personnel were given the same marching orders. My husband worked for the USAID mission; and since AID was working hard to raise the standard of living in Ethiopia, we did not have to leave.

I was teaching in the American Community School, and the news hit us around noon, as worried parents came to gather their children, request transcripts, and bid each other tearful farewells. After the school closed in confusion, I gathered my three daughters and headed home to await further developments. I drove slowly through Addis Ababa, a city I had grown to love.

As we reached the center of the city, a crowd of Ethiopians suddenly surrounded our car. I cursed my stupidity for driving my three precious children into danger. But then we realized that what the Ethiopians were saying, in broken English, was that they really did not want us to leave. They were risking government retribution to let us know we would be missed. And that was when I understood why I loved Ethiopia and why I hoped our family would be allowed to stay and try to be of some help to those beautiful people.

Another time when my heart was full and I felt a lump in my throat was after the election in South Africa. Coretta Scott King was in Johannesburg, and we gave a small dinner party in her honor. To save her travel time, we held the dinner in the Carlton Hotel, where she was staying. As the main course was being served, someone informed us that Nelson Mandela was about to make his acceptance speech in the hotel. Mrs. King was as willing as the rest of us to leave our dinners uneaten and rush to the scene of all the excitement. Never before, and surely never again, have I witnessed such a scene of jubilation. We were quickly absorbed into the crowd and found ourselves shouting and dancing and kissing and hugging friends and strangers alike.

Mr. Mandela was made aware of Mrs. King's presence and had her escorted to the stage. With their arms around each other these two nonviolent freedom fighters led the room in chanting, "Free at last, free at last, thank God Almighty, free at last." The warmth that was felt between the Americans and the South Africans who shared that evening was a feeling I will always treasure.

We were stationed in South Korea ten years after the United Nations and the United States helped South Korea fight off the invasion from North Korea. There were frequent demonstrations by students who always seemed able to find a cause to demonstrate for, or against. When the location of a demonstration was known, Americans were told by the embassy to stay away. At times someone didn't hear the warnings or there was a spontaneous demonstration we didn't know about. But we were never afraid of getting caught up in one of these, because Americans were always protected, never harmed. Both the students and the police provided this protection.

I remember a night in El Salvador when I was chased down the street after dining with a friend. My friend and I clutched our purses, sure that the two men behind us were the pickpockets we had been warned about. We were regretting not heeding warnings not to go out at night. However, the two men chasing us turned out to be our waiters from the restaurant, who wanted to return our money. They were sure we had overtipped because we didn't understand their currency. Actually, we had overtipped on purpose, because we had had such a fun evening with the waiters, who tried to figure out what to feed us and made an effort to make conversation with us when our Spanish was even more limited than their English.

Will I ever have moments like these again? Does the world still see Americans as friends? What does the world think of an American demand that they must all be for us or we will consider them against us? Does might always make right? Well, we certainly have the might. What do our friends think about our lack of interest in having clean air? Is it OK not to pay our United Nations dues? What does the world think of our bastion of democracy when we now arrest people and not notify their relatives or allow them access to lawyers? Does it seem OK to have an ever-increasing gap between the haves and the have-nots in the world? Is there nothing more we could or should do to stop the spread of HIV/AIDS? Is it OK to bully other countries into joining us in a war that might have been avoided and that might lead to a nuclear holocaust?

What exactly have I lost? Maybe I'm just imagining it. Maybe I'm just getting old and cynical. Maybe my children and grandchildren will go abroad and feel the same warmth that I once felt there. And maybe not.

My Ideal Day

Trying to write about my ideal day showed me what a greedy person I am. I can't be satisfied with less than four such days. I am too insatiable to give anything up.

On one ideal day, I would sleep late and wake up to the roar of the ocean outside my open window. I would make love before breakfast, and then have breakfast served in bed with a single red rose in a silver vase on the tray. The coffee would be so strong I could smell it long before the door opened. I would be in a luxurious hotel with my husband, and after breakfast we would have the rest of the day with nothing we had to do: we might go for a walk or a bike ride or a hike in the woods. We would go to the theater, have a late dinner, and end the day with a relaxing bath in a Jacuzzi in our hotel room. We would fall asleep with the same ocean sounds that had greeted us in the morning.

But, no, that's all wrong. On my ideal day, my husband and I would be in Cape Town, South Africa. We would have set our alarm clocks for a ridiculously early hour and thrown on some jeans and cotton shirts and grabbed the backpacks we had fixed the night before, added the food and drinks that had needed refrigeration, and set out with our favorite hiking friends to climb to the top of Table Mountain. We would feel the cool breeze, breathe deeply the clean air of the mountain, hear only the birds and our footsteps, and stop often to take in the beauty of the mountains and the ocean that we could see below us. Our friends, who know and treasure the beauty to be found here, would point out the birds and trees and flowers and views. We would stop for lunch sitting on rocks overlooking Cape Town and enjoy the food, the rest, and the easy conversation of good friends. We would spend the day climbing and at night we would fall into bed too tired to move and too happy to want to.

No, that's all wrong, too. My ideal day would be one just like today, Mother's Day. I woke up and received Mother's Day gifts and a card from my husband. We dressed and drove to the home of the youngest of our three daughters. Lori had planned the day. She knew a restaurant that served the best brunches in the world, and it was only five minutes from her home. The restaurant didn't take reservations and we would be in a hurry because my husband had an afternoon plane to catch. So, her husband would drive to the restaurant at 9:20 a.m. and put our name on the list so the rest of us could arrive at 10:00 and not have to wait. Unfortunately, when we arrived, a gloomy son-in-law announced that there would be a two-to-three-hour wait for a table for nine.

So, we moved on to plan B. The men made the rounds of other restaurants in search of a shorter wait. Because we didn't want hamburgers for breakfast, they were unsuccessful.

Plan C was invoked. At the supermarket, we picked up some eggs and waffle mix and lox and bagels and fruit and had a much better breakfast than any restaurant could offer. I rejoiced at observing how well my daughters, their husbands, and the grandchildren got along.

After our feast, I received the greatest kind of present: a homemade card with a variety of wishes and a list of theater and dance productions from which I could choose to have a ladies' night out with my girls. Talk about an ideal gift, this was it!!

All too soon it was time to return to our house so my husband could get ready for his trip. Although I will miss him, this chance to quietly write for as long as I please is surely part of any ideal day for me.

There is still a problem. On an ideal day I would surely have to have the ear of President Bush and his cabinet and the members of Congress, and I would explain to them what they are doing wrong. They would listen and mend their ways, and we would start right here in America. They would agree not to cut taxes but to increase help for our schools and health care and the needy. They would forget about star wars and, instead, fight poverty and disease overseas. They would support efforts to improve the environment and control guns. They would promise to have regular meetings with me so that I could continue to ensure that the world would become a peaceful and prosperous home for everyone. We would leave no person behind.

All ideal days end with a good night's sleep, so that is what I will do now.

Thoughts: Things Going Well

It seems easier to write when things are not going well than when life is great: to write about bad people instead of good people. If I had chosen to write about George W. Bush today, I would be scribbling away with passion. If I had chosen to write about my fear that my cancer was not destroyed, I couldn't be stopped. If I were writing about the situation in Israel or Iraq or Darfur, or children dying because of poverty, my anger and sadness would fill up my paper in no time.

So, why is it so hard to write today? Today I am happy—I love the world. I don't want to write about things that will change that feeling. What makes me so happy today is that my life for the last year has been a kind of hell for many reasons, and all those reasons are over. My surgery and chemo sent me to the hospital several times, once because I passed out and came crashing through a shower door. But at least for now, this is behind me, and everything I can do now that I couldn't do for the last year makes me so happy. Just feeling well is a new feeling that I am determined to enjoy.

When I was first ill, my husband had a hard time dealing with it, and sometimes took his frustration and sense of helplessness out on me, or really on the conditions surrounding my illness. He spent a lot of time at work or traveling, calling on my children or paying a nurse's aide to take care of me when he was away. And then, suddenly, he made a decision to do all he could for me, including actually being there, touching me, and talking to me. Now our relationship is the best it has been in many years.

My eighteen-year-old granddaughter came over to read to me; and she said, and I agree, that, while she was so sorry about my illness, she found a silver lining in the relationship we had formed in our private time together. The two daughters who live near us could not have been more helpful or caring. We all grew closer going through this family crisis. My friends in this area were there for me in a way that now makes it impossible for me to have negative thoughts about the human race. How can I rant when I am surrounded by fantastic people?

My daughter in Israel and friends and relatives outside of the Washington, D.C., area came through with cards, phone calls, and gifts. I am still in wonder at the constant flood of care and affection that I have received during my illness.

I have been worried about my Israeli daughter and her husband and children during this latest Middle East crisis. But now there is a cease-fire and they can go out and not worry about Katyusha rockets. That gives me one more reason to be happy.

Several American states have given up on the federal government and are starting to take over some of the tasks one would assume the federal government would take care of. Realizing that global warming is real and must be dealt with, individual states are signing treaties not only with each other but with foreign countries, in order to lessen the pollution they are creating. The governors, including Republican governors, have worked together to send a letter to Congress to stop the administration's attempt to give the president control over all national guard units if the president declares a national emergency. So there is hope that Americans have figured out that this administration is evil and will not continue to let them get away with it.

No one knows, thank goodness, what the future holds, but that seems to me all the more reason to allow myself to be happy when I can!

Poems

The Veldt

In the summer the ground is parched
and cracks with thirst
and there are no pretty flowers here.

In the winter the cold wind
bites through layers of clothes
and I ask, can this be Africa?

Then why does my soul seek *this* place
when I have loved the heaving oceans
and felt the awe of wind-swept mountains?

Here I see an acacia tree
lonely and stark it stands
against the vibrant sunset.

Here I lie on a cot in a tent
and listen in my sleep
and hope to hear a hungry lion roar.

Here the Africans speak English
so softly it sounds sweet
and live with ease beside the animals we fear.

Here the giraffes walk with dignity
their curiosity brings them near
and so we stare at one another till they get bored and leave.

Here a herd of buffalo surrounds our open jeep
their huge dark shapes move slowly by
they pay us no heed—we do not count for much.

Here with no electric lights
the stars can all be seen
and nature can't be fooled.

Here the lions kill a baby zebra
the hyena eat the bones
the mother comes and mourns her child.

Here impala graze so peacefully
and elephants teach their young
and countless types of birds fly above us all.

Here the female leopard hides her cub within a cave
she can only hope he will survive
'til she makes her kill and comes for him.

Here the monkeys play and chatter in the trees
and those sleepy looking hippos
kill more people then the rest.

And I will never get enough
Of this harsh paradise.

A Villanelle?

This world we know, so full of good and bad
No way to tilt to the peace we'd love
And deep within we find we're feeling sad

Nature gives such beauty to make us glad
And we feel awed by oceans and mountains
This world we know, so full of good and bad

Man creates such horror and we've been had
Billions for war, but none for the people
And deep within we find we're feeling sad

Yet people give and fight to set things right
Then nature sends tsunamis and earthquakes
This world we know, so full of good and bad

We can't trust nature; we can't trust man
But still we find our souls are full of joy
And deep within we find we're feeling sad

We all must rage at things that make us mad
And love the wonders that we see each day
This world we know, so full of good and bad
And deep within we find we're feeling sad

My Color

I think I may be yellow
Full of mischief, full of fun
Dancing with a sunbeam
Running barefoot through daffodils
Yes, I think I may be yellow
Or I could be colorless, maybe nothing at all

I think I may be red
Full of passion, full of life
Dancing wildly all the night
Galloping bareback through the day
Yes, I think I may be red
Or I could be colorless, maybe nothing at all

I think I may be brown
Soft as kittens, gentle as dew
Comfy as my worn-out slippers
Sleeping and dreaming on a bed of moss
Yes, I think I may be brown
Or I could be colorless, maybe nothing at all

Wives of Great Men

by E. Laura Goldberg

For Helen

Wives of great men
are shaded out
under boughs
of huge spouses.

They grow their own blossoms.

Only those who search
among the undergrowth
will come upon them,
and marvel at their loveliness.

www.ingramcontent.com/pod-product-compliance
Lightning Source LLC
Chambersburg PA
CBHW020510100426
42813CB00030B/3184/J